RAILS OVER THE ANDES

By the same author:

Footsteps of the Celts by Rail, Book Guild Publishing, 2009
From Bangkok to Siberia Via the Marrakech Express, Book Guild Publishing, 2011

RAILS OVER THE ANDES

A Journey through Peru, Colombia and Ecuador

William Bleasdale

Book Guild Publishing
Sussex, England

To the memory of my parents
John Duckworth Bleasdale
Annie Bleasdale

Contents

Peru

I had long wanted to do one of the great railway journeys of the world and although there are plenty to choose from, the combination of the highest standard gauge railway in the world (15,693 feet above sea level) coupled with the diversity and cultural history of Peru meant that there was really only one choice as far as I was concerned.

Most people know about the historic Inca city of Machu Picchu and its accessibility only by rail, but I wanted to do more than just that. I wanted to cover the entire rail system of Peru not only for the pleasure of travelling by train over that amazing system but also to see the country and its people at first hand.

I had already studied a map of Peru and could see that most of the rail system passed through areas that were rarely visited by tourists. Over a period of eighteen months I contacted several companies that not only specialised in Latin American travel but were also able to tailor in individual requirements. I soon discovered that my project was not going to be an easy one, as it transpired that more than sixty per cent of Peru's railway system is for freight only (including the highest point), and those companies that I contacted were unable to carry people on those lines.

I had almost reached the point of giving up when I noticed a very small advertisement in a Saturday national newspaper. It was for railway holidays, and I telephoned for a brochure without much hope of it being very much different from the many others that I had already seen.

I have the brochure open in front of me as I write up these notes, and at the time I could hardly believe that, after so many disappointments, I had found a company that offered travel over the entire Peruvian rail system, as well as the opportunity to visit several historic attractions.

The fifteen-day tour that they were offering turned out to be a magical experience, and I hope that with my notes, pictures and memory I can do justice to it.

Saturday, 4 October 2003, and I am up at 1.30 a.m. to catch the 6.10 flight to Amsterdam, from where we will fly to Lima, with a stop en route at Bonaire.

This will be the first of many early starts over the next two weeks.

We arrive at Amsterdam at 8.15 a.m. and it is pouring with rain. Schiphol Airport is a vast place, and I enter into an almost endless walkway with shops and gates on either side. It seems like I have walked miles to reach gate E2, but everything is very well signed and there are automated walkways (all working) and electric cars for the disabled and the less energetic. It makes Manchester seem quite homely and small.

There are seventeen of us travelling and we are due to meet our tour manager at the transit area, where we will be identified by our distinctive green luggage labels. These have a picture of a locomotive on them, of course!

I spot a label and it turns out to be our tour manager. He is busy trying to spot other labels. The members of our group are travelling from airports all over England, and he is keen to ensure that he has a full tally.

I meet some of the group but there is not much time to get to know anyone as we are being asked to board. The plane is a DB11 Tri-star and it is full. I wonder, as always, how a thing that size leaves the ground with hundreds of passengers and their luggage on board. Too much imagination!

We leave thirty minutes late and I try to settle for the nine hours' flying time to Lima. The legroom is very poor for a long-haul flight, particularly as the woman passenger in front of me seems determined to put her seat back as far as it will go.

The cabin crew have apparently resolved that we will not arrive hungry or thirsty, as we are continually being offered food or drink, or both.

There is a one-hour stop at Bonaire in the Netherlands Antilles for refuelling. Some passengers are leaving here and some are joining. I take the chance to stretch my legs and get some fresh air. It is like a wall of hot air as we leave the air-conditioned comfort of the plane, the airport thermometer says 36°C. The airport is very small and there is nothing to do except stand around in a café area. It is however, a chance to have a chat with some of the others in the group.

It is three and a half hours' flying time to Lima from here. That will make it a total of twelve and a half hours from Amsterdam. We are now six hours behind UK time.

Arrive at Lima 6.30 p.m. local time. The temperature is 27°C. We meet Stuart, who is the owner of the company making the arrangements in Peru. He will be with us throughout the tour. He is a Spanish-speaking Englishman and moved here fourteen years ago when he met and married a local girl.

The transfer to the Hotel Plaza del Bosque is very efficient; this will be our base for the next two nights. I have a very nice suite with double bedroom, fitted kitchen, bathroom and lounge, but it is now about 8.30 p.m. and my only thought is bed. I remember to ring home at 9 p.m. to report safe arrival, forgetting that it is 3 a.m. in the UK!

The next morning I am up and down for breakfast at 6.45. I am the only one there. The selection and display of food is excellent, particularly the fruit, of which there seems to be many kinds. I settle for fruit juice, fresh pineapple chunks, ham and local fresh bread. I later discover that boiled eggs are available but you have to ask for them. I have already tried out my limited Spanish, and although I know the Spanish for eggs, the request to have them boiled almost defeats me. The waiter is very patient and the eggs, when they come, are done to perfection.

After breakfast I stroll outside the hotel and meet with a

policeman. He does not speak any English but smiles a lot and is very friendly and although the language is very limited it is an excellent cultural exchange!

It is now 9.30, and we are all assembling by our coach for the Lima tour that will include the city centre, the port and the rail yard.

First stop is the port and entrance to the rail yard. Just inside the gates is a small steam engine on a plinth, number TPC10, and there is much excitement among the group. It is a very small loco and has obviously not seen service for some considerable time … and to be honest it does not stir me very much.

There is much talking and arm-waving between our guide and the port security staff, but it still turns out that we are not going to be allowed entry. We are allowed to have a group photo in front of the loco before we depart to find the other entrance to the yard.

The port does not seem very interesting but I suppose all ports look the same.

We have found the other entrance to the rail yard and the official in charge is only too pleased to be able to show us around.

We can also climb all over the Beyer Peacock 1953 steam loco, number 206, which had been scheduled for part of our journey tomorrow; unfortunately this is not possible as it seems to have developed a leak in its water tank.

There are several diesel locos which have originated from Mexico, Canada and Brazil and we can also see 1001, the big 4,000HP diesel that will pull our train tomorrow. The tour around the workshops is very interesting as nearly all the equipment is British made and some of it is over a hundred years old and still in use!

We have moved on and are having lunch at a restaurant called Mango's. It is built on the edge of a cliff overlooking the Pacific and the view is superb, just a long sweep of beach with white-capped Pacific rollers along its full length. I have taken a photograph but the combination of sea mist and heat haze may not allow me to do justice to what is a magnificent view.

The Pacific from Mango's Restaurant

My next treat is choosing from a wide range of delicious-looking traditional dishes of Peru, and I fall back on the help of Stuart, our guide and interpreter, as I am determined to try as many Peruvian dishes as I can over the next two weeks. I eventually settle for three, *rocoto relleno* (hot pepper stuffed with meat), *ceviche* (selection of raw fish marinated in lemon, chilli and onions) and *lomo saltado* (sauteed beef in onions and sauce). I am too full to try any of the magnificent-looking desserts, but the lunch still turns out to be the first of many superb meals that I enjoy over the next two weeks.

The coach has taken us into the centre of Lima and we now have about two hours to look around. There are thousands of people in and around the Plaza Mayor and it is impossible to get into the central square. It is the Festival of the Rosary where the people celebrate one year ending and another beginning. The Cathedral is decorated from top to bottom with long flowing drapes of purple and white and there are many people dressed in flowing purple cloaks with a white rope around their middle.

5

Plaza Mayor, Lima

As we round a corner, we find the road surface decorated from one side to the other with flowers of many colours that depict religious messages and images. Although there are many police, they are unobtrusive and the atmosphere is one of happiness and wellbeing.

We are heading for an ancient convent that is still in use. The courtyard in front is packed with many stalls most of which seem to be selling food, perhaps understandable on the day, although there are some selling religious souvenirs. Some of the stalls are selling huge chunks of roast pig. It looks quite tempting until I see a small child, with extremely dirty fingers, picking at one of the carcasses, and I decide that I am not that hungry.

Inside the convent it is very quiet and although I am not particularly religious, I can appreciate the beauty and tranquillity of the surroundings. We are taken down into the catacombs. It is

6

quite eerie down here and I have to stoop to walk most of the time. There are many bones and skulls, all neatly arranged in rows or circles.

We also have an opportunity to see the frontage of the railway station, it is spotlessly clean, and its lemon and white stonework gleams in the bright sun. It is topped with balustrade, carvings and a clock, guarded by two statues, with the words 'Ferrocarril Central' underneath: very impressive.

Desamparados Station

Afterwards we make our way to the meeting point for the coach, and as we are waiting on a street corner I am approached by a woman who tries to sell me five *chupa* lollies for two soles (about 40p). When I say, 'No, thank you,' she assumes that I am American and immediately changes the price to one dollar!

In poor Spanish I try to explain that I shouldn't eat sweets and I emphasise this by rubbing my stomach. Some men standing close by (dressed in immaculate black suits) assume, I think, that I mean *her* stomach and there is much laughter. The whole situation then dissolves into much hilarity, including the woman, although I can't be sure that we are all laughing at the same thing.

The coach has now taken us to Lima's famous Gold Museum. The museum is actually some distance from Lima itself and is in a tranquil garden setting with a few discreet souvenir shops. At ten soles, I can't resist a replica Inca sacrificial knife.

The contents of the museum were originally started as a private collection and the former owner's house is in the museum grounds. There are many thousands of items, and guns and armaments appear to outnumber the gold exhibits many times. There are also some exhibits of sacrificial heads taken as trophies.

The gold museum could have been much more interesting if the items had been labelled with more information. It was disappointing not to be able to see how old a thing was or where it was found.

It is now dark and we have returned to our hotel for dinner and an early night, for me at any rate, as it is a 5 a.m. start tomorrow.

It is 5.45 a.m. and we are at Desamparados Station. There is a long freight train, headed by 1001, and at the back are our two coaches. The incongruity of tacking two coaches on to the end of a freight train is amazing. You can never imagine it happening in the UK!

One of the coaches is open-plan, comfortably upholstered, and the other is a gem of an observation car that is also fitted out with a bathroom, kitchen and a bedroom. It is mostly made of teak, almost certainly Victorian, and a wonder to behold.

There are many introductions and much hand-shaking, and we eventually leave Lima half an hour late. At this point, enter Percy. Percy is working freelance for Stuart's company, Tucano Reps, and will be with us for most of the fortnight making a video of the trip. He is some way down the platform from the train when it suddenly decides to leave and he is forced to make a run for it, video camera and all. Even though it is a freight train he only just makes it; I am glad, for he turned out to be a great companion over the next two weeks.

The line out of Lima is hemmed in on both sides by very poor buildings that seem to stretch for miles. The locomotive horn is continually blaring to warn of our coming as people are continually crossing backwards and forwards across the track.

Half an hour since we left Lima Station, and there are still miles and miles of shanty town, dilapidated buildings and poverty; and we in the UK worry about whether our bins get emptied on the right day! It certainly puts that into perspective. Everything looks very brown, dusty and dry; our guide says that it never rains in Lima at all. The coaches at this point are really rocking; it must say something for the state of the track, as we are not going at any great speed.

There are some fascinating images along the way. There is a group of people sitting beside a table under a tent while a woman on the other side is boiling up a strange-looking white liquid in a large black pot; some of the men are eating this with every sign of enjoyment. There are two dogs barking madly outside a house when suddenly a woman comes out with a bowl of water and hurls it all over them. The modes of transport are quite fascinating, and I see several motorbikes that have two wheels at the back with a seat and a cover over the top, a bit like the three-wheelers in India. Suddenly, two women of twenty-something come out of one of the mud brick houses, they are absolutely immaculately dressed and made up and would not have looked out of place walking down any city high street; the contrast with their surroundings is stark.

We are just passing Santa Clara. At the track side there is an old Dormobile without windows and a family living in it. Some people have made an effort to brighten up the front of their houses with small trees and grass but the backdrop remains the same, even though it is now nearly forty-five minutes since we left Lima station. There are a few banana trees, but they look rather dry and tired and I can't imagine them having bananas on them. I have just seen a woman washing plates and clothes in a filthy-looking stream; it's amazing what we worry about at home. Others are scavenging for anything useful in a rubbish tip. Is this the price that they pay for leaving the countryside and coming to the big city to be better off?

We have just passed a large brown gate in front of some sort of compound. On it in large letters is '*Virgen de Chapisca*' … I am sure that it does not mean what I think it means.

The train has just ground to a sudden halt and there are crowds of people running. I think we may have hit somebody on a crossing. Ten minutes later and there are still crowds of people and vehicles clustered around the locomotive. We have now reversed off the crossing and an ambulance has turned up. Ten minutes later and we are on our way; the news is that we have run over a lady and she has been killed. It's incredible to think that after an incident like that we should be on our way after only twenty minutes.

The locomotive horn is continuing to blare.

We are just passing a school. It is 7.30 a.m. and the children are already arriving. A car is driving slowly alongside us with two dogs chasing it and trying to chew the bumper.

The sun has now broken through the haze and we are suddenly much higher, about halfway between Santa Clara and Chosica, where we are due to make a five-minute stop. The scenery is now much more rural, and there are lots of bananas, sweet corn and other crops. There is also a backdrop of lovely mountains.

Chosica is quite a big station with sidings, engine shed, rail depot and a turntable. The whole station area is clean, tidy and well looked after. It is very pretty with flowers and there is an identical observation coach to ours in a bay platform. It seems a tragedy that it doesn't serve passengers any more.

*   *   *

10

We have left Chosica and are still climbing; it is now about 1,200 metres. There is a lovely view up front with a range of mountains shrouded in haze; looking at the view ahead it is difficult to imagine that there is a way through. The locomotive continues to blare its horn as we pass another road crossing. It echoes, and bouncing back off the mountains that now completely surround us, and is a spectacular noise.

A little rural village and there is somebody making what I think are mats from bamboo. It turns out that they are the walls of the little dwellings that they live in.

We have reached San Bartolomé, where No. 206 had been scheduled to take over as far as San Isidro. This is a place that people come to visit (by road) to enjoy the view and local surroundings; another immaculate unused station.

San Bartolome

There is a zigzag here and there is much movement to get the coaches and loco in the right order for the next leg. There is a turntable with its pit half full of water but it has obviously been

Changes at San Bartolome

worked many times before and works OK today, and we are on our way again.

I am enjoying a ride in the cab from this point, and some of the views are very special, if not scary. We are approaching a bridge at Puente Carrión and the cab view is quite something. I would have to think twice about walking over it, never mind taking a heavy freight train over the bridge. Perhaps I worry too much, but the drop is quite something. As we enter one of the many tunnels, we disturb a colony of bats, and as we pass through, the locomotive headlight shows that the air is quite literally black with them. Shortly afterwards I see the wrecks of wagons and carriages that have fallen down the valley at some time ... best not to think about it too much.

The sheer height and grandeur of the mountains is breathtaking and the whole experience from the front of the loco is quite wonderful.

* * *

12

Puente Carrion

It is about 11 a.m. and we have just ground to a halt at a point about halfway between Surco and Matucana. It is a passing place, and is one of the remotest places that I have ever seen. As I look out of the window I see what appears to be most of the engineering train staff climbing the mountainside. It turns out that there is a train ahead of us, heading in the opposite direction, that has become derailed, and as it is about 500 feet directly above us, the climb is the quickest way, although I wouldn't fancy it as we are now at about 6,500 feet above sea level.

I get the impression that we could be stuck here for some time, although I am sure that the railway staff are well used to situations like this. Looking at the map, we are about halfway to Oroya, where we are due to stop overnight. On the journey between here and Oroya we still have to climb another 9,000 feet before we reach the highest rail point in the world at Ticlio, 4,782 metres above sea level.

It is very hot.

Time passes slowly, but the only person who seems bothered is

13

Mike, who says that it will now be dark when we reach the highest point at Ticlio. People are just sitting and chatting, while others are casually strolling around.

Occasionally there is the blast of a locomotive horn from above and a ripple of anticipation from below, but they are all false alarms. Then suddenly, three hours later news comes that they have managed to re-rail the locomotive.

We shunt into the passing loop and fifteen minutes later the other train appears and we are on our way. I make the comment that these things usually come in threes, little realising what a prophecy it will be.

Two hours and several zigzags later and we are stuck up a mountain, on a zigzag, at 11,000 feet with a broken coupling on our front coach. I have been called Jonah by my friends back at home when I go to watch our local football team!

We all stand around and look at the coupling very wisely, but it is obvious that the dropped coupling needs to be replaced. The train staff talk and think about it for a while and eventually radio for assistance.

Stuart wants to report ahead that we will be very late but he can't get a signal on his mobile phone. It is very cold up here and people are in fleece coats and jumpers. Strangely, I am not feeling the cold, following a recent operation, and Stuart says that his memory of the incident will not be a broken coupling but me walking around, in almost arctic cold, in shirtsleeves.

At one side of the track the mountain sheers up and on the other there is a drop of several hundred feet to the river and road below. The edge is quite close to the track and it concentrates the mind when you are walking about! There is a coach caught in a pool of sunlight on the road below and from here it looks like a toy.

This road is a good quality tarmac surface and has followed us virtually all the way from Lima; it is the reason for the demise of

It's a long way down

passengers on this section of line, as it became much cheaper to travel on the bus when the road had been completed. I ask where the money for the road came from, as it must have been a very difficult and expensive project. It turns out the railway paid for it!

It seems that the government, some time ago, privatised some sections of the railway system in Peru and the money from that was used to pay for the construction of this, and other, roads in Peru.

Two hours have now passed and the rescue squad have arrived with a new pin. Forty-five minutes later and we are on our way, but will not arrive at the highest point for another one and a half hours yet, by which time it will be quite dark. The group photo will probably not happen.

We are now on our way, and although the light is now very poor I have just taken a photo of a bridge up ahead because of the combination of rail, road and river.

15

We pass through Chicla at about 6.30 and eventually arrive at Ticlio at about 8 p.m. It is pitch-dark, very cold (but not for me!), and there is snow up here, even though it is spring. To be at the highest point on the world rail system is quite a moment, but the darkness and the cold do not encourage us to linger for more than a few minutes. I feel that I must take at least one picture and manage to grab a shot of Percy as he walks past; I doubt if there will be much else in the shot, and this later turns out to be true.

Percy

We eventually arrive at Oroya at 10.15 p.m. (sixteen hours later) and transfer to a coach for the journey to Tarma, where we are staying the night. We arrive at the hotel at 11.45 p.m., and at midnight some of the party (including me) are sitting down to dinner!

I am up again at 3.30 a.m. and at 5 a.m. I am sitting down to breakfast. The coach is due to pick us up at 5.30 a.m. for our train, to Huancayo, to leave at 7.20 a.m.

Tarma is situated in a large deep valley and has its own micro-climate, so much so, that virtually all the flowers that are grown in Peru for export to the USA and Europe are grown here! Locals call Tarma 'The Pearl of the Andes'.

As we make our way along the valley floor and up its steep and winding sides, we can see the evidence, for there are banks and rows of fresh flowers everywhere. It is spring, and we are probably seeing the valley at its best time.

Because of its climate and beautiful surroundings, Tarma is also a very popular place for local people, from a wide area, to visit.

When people talk about late nights and early mornings, I can now tell them a thing or two, although the amazing thing is that, as I stand on Oroya Station at 6.30 the following morning, I don't feel particularly tired!

It is a beautiful day, hot and clear.

At 7 a.m. the train slowly winds its way out of the town, and as it does it passes close by several industrial plants and the view is not pretty. It is dirty and unpleasantly odorous, but as Oroya is the industrial capital of Peru it is to be expected, and industry has to go somewhere!

We are soon out of the town area and surrounded by brown and grey mountains that have a very Ice Age appearance about them. There is a river flowing alongside us which will stay with us for many miles. There is no sign of any greenery, and if it wasn't for the river, we could be travelling over the surface of a dead planet.

Two hours later and the surroundings are just beginning to change. We are passing isolated mud houses but with very little evidence of crops or animals. It appears to be truly subsistence living at this point.

The view is beginning to slowly change and there are now trees, grass and some stunted bushes as we cross a bridge at Mal Paso and follow the river from the other side.

We pass through three small stations without stopping: Pilchaca at 9.05 a.m., Cuenca at 9.20 a.m. and Tambo at 9.30; they may

Mal Paso

be closed stations but it is often difficult to tell. At Tambo we take one angle of a large railway triangle where there is a short spur to Jauja; I am not sure if it is still operational.

The isolated houses now become small communities and the valley has widened out into a vast plain with evidence of cultivation everywhere.

There are very few clouds and the sky is incredibly blue.

On both sides of the train there are many crops and trees. There are people working in the fields and everywhere is suddenly very green. There is very little evidence of mechanisation and the men and women are working with either hand tools or their bare hands. Here and there are tethered cows and women with blanket bundles walking along ploughed furrows.

Some of the houses have compounds made from mud bricks, in which the people keep their animals, presumably at night, and I notice that the tops of the walls have cactus plants growing in them. Is this the equivalent of our barbed wire?

The contrast with the view of the last two hours is very striking.

These pronounced contrasts and changes will continue to be a feature of the journey over the next two weeks, and will be part of the many facets of this magnificent country that I experience.

The scene changes again and the area becomes quite wooded. They are all eucalyptus trees, which the local people harvest. There is nothing wasted as the leaves are used for either feed or animal bedding, while the young branches are used for fence and house construction. The eucalyptus trees grow well in this country and are felled in such a way that they come again from the bottom and can then be used again in two or three years' time.

The train is slowing down but it turns out that the driver is merely giving someone a lift to Huancayo!

The view has changed again to the wide plain, only now there is a river flowing alongside again and what seems like hundreds of people washing blankets in the river and laying them out in the sun to dry. It has probably been done this way for hundreds of years.

We passed San Jeronimo a few minutes ago, and are now in the urban sprawl of the outskirts of Huancayo. There are lots of ponchos, wide-brimmed hats and flared-out skirts. There are no paved streets in these outskirts and all the buildings look ramshackle.

The difference between urban and country life has been shown very vividly on the trip from Oroya to Huancayo. The line from Lima to Oroya was certainly breathtaking; but, to me, that trip through the long valley and plain has shown a wonderful picture of typically Peruvian life beyond the urban areas, and I feel privileged to have seen it.

The rail distance from Lima to Huancayo is 215 miles.

Huancayo Station is no longer open to passengers, but the town does have a railway station; it is narrow gauge and is the next leg of our trip, this time to Huancavelica. The line up to this point has been standard gauge and there is a length of dual gauge track running through the town for about a mile and connecting the two stations.

The station is clean and smartly painted but no longer used by passengers! The locomotive drops our two coaches and begins shunting its freight wagons, while we start to explore. In front of the platform there is large expanse of grass with several lines running through it, there is also a large triangle for turning locos and trains; it also leads to a rail shed (closed). There is a steam locomotive parked on one of the lines that has obviously not been in use for some time, although it has clearly been maintained, as the grease points have recently been attended to. The locomotive's number is 112 and it has on its tender in big letters the words 'Ferrocarril Huancayo Huancavelica', and underneath, 'Municipalidad Provincial Huancayo'. It looks in very good condition and it is a shame that it is apparently no longer used.

Huancayo Station

There is an organised trip to the rail works at Huancayo's narrow gauge station and everybody is piling into a minibus, I decide not to go as it is very hot and the minibus seems very claustrophobic to me. I opt for sitting in our coach and reading, and find that Bernadette had decided to do the same. Bernadette does not appear to be feeling very well and we fall into conversation. She says that she has not come on this trip because of the trains, but because of the trip itself and the unusual areas that we are scheduled to travel to.

It is hot in the coach.

After lunch we make the transfer to our hotel, which is situated on the main square. The entrance foyer and dining room have a somewhat dated air, but my room, although a bit basic, is comfortable and spacious.

Some of us decide to go for stroll around the town centre.

It is very busy and there are lots of people about and we attract quite a bit of attention, this is almost certainly because we are off the beaten track for tourists and there are no other 'white faces' to be seen. There is no sense of apprehension on our part as the people are very friendly and smile in greeting; this includes the shoeshine boys, who pursue us for a while.

After a while I leave the group and head back to the hotel. It is about 4 p.m. and I feel hot and in need of a sit-down; I think the effects of the altitude are starting to get to me.

Here in Huancayo we are at 10,699 feet above sea level.

I head straight for my room and stretch out on the bed. The room seems very hot and airless, even with the window and door open. I drink water continually for the next three hours and try to sleep, but every time I close my eyes a sense of claustrophobia comes on me. At eight o'clock I give in and ask Stuart if he can get me a doctor, who arrives quite quickly and gives me a thorough examination. My blood pressure is low and his diagnosis is that I am suffering from a combination of tiredness and altitude sickness. He prescribes some pills for the symptoms of altitude sickness and urges me to rest. Stuart is with the doctor and they both comment on the extreme coldness in the room, but to me it seems very hot. The doctor charges me sixty soles (about £12) and I consider it a bargain.

The next morning I am feeling much better and join the others for breakfast. There's not a lot of choice, really, for our train is due to leave at 7 a.m.

Chilca Station is an amazing sight. The entrance area is thronged with people selling food, drink, fruit, ponchos, hats and trinkets; in fact, you name it and it appears to be on sale! There is even a makeshift café outside with a bench and table, where people are taking an early breakfast.

Inside the long open booking hall it is absolutely packed with people waiting for the train. There are sellers of cigarettes, jewellery, shoelaces and other necessities moving among them. There is a buzz of sound from many conversations, and I try my Spanish on three women close by. Their dress is very traditional although the hats are all in different styles, from a little flowery thing with a chin strap to a pink boater to a black stovepipe. They have many blanket bundles with them. 'Stovepipe' wraps her green shawl around her and turns her back on me, as she does not like the camera, but the other two giggle with pleasure at what is obviously a great novelty for them.

Huancayo Station

On one of the walls are two large murals. One of them illustrates a train crossing a high girder bridge mounted on what appears to

22

be the foundations of an old Inca bridge, and the other is a geographical map of the line to Huancavelica showing all the stations.

Suddenly the gates are opened and there is a great surge forward. Although there are about twelve carriages on the train I am glad that we have one reserved, as there seem to be hundreds of people trying to get on.

There is much shunting as the locomotive rearranges his train so that there are two wooden box cars immediately behind, followed by our carriage, followed by the rest of the train, they then decide that two more carriages are needed.

Fellow passengers at Huancayo

During the shunting we are suddenly alongside a carriage full of young girls of about thirteen or fourteen, they become wildly excited when I point my camera at them and try to get heads and arms outside the small windows to wave and smile.

The train is now so long that the front of it is outside the gates (stations are fenced and gated; these gates are shut and locked when there are no trains). There is also security even when the stations do not serve passengers; this is obviously why the stations that we have seen have been in such good condition, even though they have not been used for some considerable time.

The process seems to take a long while but is in fact only about ten minutes and we leave at 7.10 a.m.

As the train makes its way through the suburbs of Huancayo there is activity everywhere. At every road crossing there are cars and vans waiting sometimes patiently, sometimes not so patiently! There is a lot of people movement, except those enjoying their morning breakfast at the railside café. These cafés are in the open air and are usually a table and a couple of benches presided over by a woman in charge of a Primus stove. It is a wonderful picture of everyday life in this part of Peru and the people are very ready to smile and wave.

It seems a privilege that they are willing, with a smile, to share their country with a stranger who points a camera at them.

Very soon we are travelling alongside the River Mantaro. It flows through a wide plain and there are eucalyptus trees on one side and cultivated areas on the other. This view continues for a few miles and we then begin to climb. Suddenly we are in a high-sided valley with trees on both sides of the river. There are mountains all around and the brightness of the sun and cloudless sky is quite dazzling.

The river is now much narrower and flowing more rapidly. In between some of the trees there are some cultivated areas, some lush with a crop of something very green-leaved, while other fields are brown as they wait for the crop to appear.

The view changes again and we are now perched high above the river which tumbles on its way with much white water. The sides of the gorge are very steep, and the ledge has been hewn out of one side of the mountain to accommodate the railway, which twists and turns as it follows the course of the river. Sometimes the last carriage is almost opposite the first one!

Occasionally there are some flat areas at the side of the line and we have just passed several cultivated fields with dry-stone walls and mud-brick houses with tiled roofs. The houses are much bigger and in better condition than a lot of those that we have seen so far. The brightness and heat of the sun is reflecting back from the opposite side of the gorge.

We are still climbing and the river is now far below.

It is 8.45 a.m. and we have just reached our first stop at Man Telleria. Here, we are at 9,862 feet above sea level, and have fifty-two miles still to go to Huancavelica.

Unlike the line we've travelled for the last two days, the line from Huancayo to Huancavelica is open to passengers and well used by them. Two people get off here and there are several men and two small boys sheltering in the shade of the stone-built station. The two boys are keen to have their photograph taken.

In keeping with many of the dwellings alongside the line that we have seen so far, one of them is painted, in large letters, with what appears to be a political campaign slogan. The house is in poor condition but these things don't appear to be important to the local people or, more probably, they lack the resources to do anything about it.

There is a cluster of houses, some with mud-brick walled enclosures that contain crops of vegetables or prickly pear.

The whole landscape is a mixture of brown and green and there is now a narrow dirt-track road on the opposite side of the mountain.

Half an hour later and we have reached Cuenca. There is a mud-walled shelter and a stone-built platform and nothing else. All around are high mountains, and a lot of people get off the train here. As I watch an old woman with a large blanket bundle on her back struggling up the hillside at the back of the station I wonder where on earth they are going, as there are no signs of any habitation. There are now some fluffy white clouds but the sky is still a vivid blue and it is quite hot.

The activity at Cuenca is nothing compared to that at our next stop, which is at Aguas Calientes. This is an area of great charm and beauty and there are open-air hot springs within a large grassed area alongside the railway. There are several beautiful trees to shade under, or tree stumps inviting you to sit and enjoy the view. The mountains shimmer green and blue in the sunshine and the green blue water of the pools invite you in.

Aguas Calientes Station

It is a popular spot for visitors from Huancayo and other towns, and it is here that we are going to drop the last four carriages of our train. These contain the young people whom we saw in Huancayo, and they are here for a day out to enjoy the hot springs and other amenities. Interesting that they keep their carriages here for the return journey; they will certainly be sure of a seat!

We will be here for a few minutes and a lot of people take the opportunity to get off the train and walk around. The train crew need to contact someone and I get my first view of the country's telephone system in operation. It consists of a field telephone and a man with a pole that has a metal hook at the end with a wire leading down the pole. While one man operates the phone, the other drapes the pole over the telephone line that runs alongside the track, and the connection is made! Simple, but effective.

Making a phone call, Peru style

Twenty minutes later and we are in Izcuchaca. Here we are 9,465 feet above sea level and just over halfway to Huancavelica. This is a town of some importance and outward prosperity. It is also a passing place for trains and we have a few minutes to wait for a train going the other way.

There is a very busy market by the station and the place is a mass of colour with all the different fruits and vegetables on offer.

There is great interest in the arrival of both us and the train, and I feel sure that not many Europeans pass this way. The station itself is extremely smart, with trees, gardens and a neatly paved platform with seats. Many people are leaving and joining the train here and the place is vibrant. To add to the general air of hustle and bustle, there is man fighting to control a pig that is on the end of a long rope.

Izcuchaca Station

There are stone buildings in the colonial style to the back of the station and these include a bank and a church. As we leave the station I can see a school of some size.

Although Izcuchaca is obviously a place of some prosperity there is a contrast as an old woman struggles down a narrow rough track on the opposite side of the railway; she has already made two perilous journeys with boxes and now has a large blanket bundle on her back.

A little way from the station and on the same side, there are some houses built on top of a bank which, to me, looks very unstable. They are however of some quality, with trees and verandas, and they are brightly painted.

The backdrop of towering mountains around Izcuchaca is very impressive.

We have reached Mariscal Caceres, and it is quite different here. Although a lot of the buildings are stone and plaster, some with ornate balconies, there is general air of somnolence, together with a lack of customers at the line-side shop.

Not long after Mariscal Caceres the river swings away to the left and we plunge into a tunnel on our way to the next stop at Station 88. This is a little halt just before Acoria, and I assume that its name comes from the fact that it is 88 kilometres from Huancayo.

In the event we don't stop here, and apart from the continuing impressive scenery there is nothing much else to see.

Just before we reach Acoria we are, again, joined by a river. It is not very deep and, with trees on either bank, it tumbles its way over rocks. There is a woman at the waterside scrubbing clothes and drying them on the bank. It is a very colourful scene, with the blue-green water, brown and grey rocks, blue sky and the red, blue, yellow and black of her washing. In some way that I can't explain I find the whole scene very fulfilling; perhaps the perspective of the woman is different! Or then, perhaps not!

Acoria is 10,400 feet above sea level and twenty miles from Huancavelica. Again the station is busy. The railway and the communities between Huancayo and Huancavelica interact and are dependent on each other, and long may it continue. We used to have a railway system like that in the UK until the strange decision was taken years ago to trim the branch lines from the main lines. Like a tree, the trunk can only wither from such treatment.

At the side of the station there is a plinth on which there is a large stone book; unfortunately, I was unable to establish what the significance of it was.

We are now running through the outlying area of Yauli, 11,106 feet above sea level and just ten miles from Huancavelica. The station is very neatly paved and has lighting columns, the first that I have seen. Despite the attention that has been lavished on the station it is not busy and only two people get on.

There are now more fluffy white clouds and the sky is a beautiful blue. As I look back the way that we have come there is a sense of peace and timelessness about the view.

We reach Estación Huancavelica: journey's end for the time being, and 12,073 feet above sea level.

The arrival of the train is a major event, and apart from the many people leaving the train, there are many more locals who have come to meet friends and family, to sell something or just to look – including those that peer into the train to see who is left!

I find it very sad that this part of our journey through Peru is finished.

The journey from Huancayo to Huancavelica over eighty miles of twisting narrow gauge track all at over 10,000 feet above sea level, must surely contain all the best ingredients of an exciting rail journey: towering mountains, deep gorges, rushing torrents, remote and fascinating communities, lush valleys, the sound and feel of a 4,000 horsepower locomotive pulling twelve packed carriages, the interaction between passengers and those on the station at every stop, beautiful blue sky and an ever-changing landscape, a seemingly endless supply of things to photograph, and – last but certainly not least – the feeling of being part of something very different but very special.

Huancavelica Station

Welcome to Huancavelica

I'm not sure if I recorded all the stations on this line, but the following is a list of those that I did see, with arrival times. Starting from Huancayo:

Rettamatoc: 8 a.m.
Ingarama: 8.10 a.m.
Man Telleria: 8.40 a.m.
Pilchaca: 9.05 a.m.
Cuenca: 9.20 a.m.
Aguas Calientes: 9.40 a.m.
La Menta: 9.55 a.m.
Izcuchaca: 10 a.m.
Mariscal Caceres: 10.20 a.m.
Station 88: 11.20 a.m.
Acoria: 11.30 a.m.
Yauli: 12.20 p.m.
Huancavelica: 1 p.m.

Mountains tower on all sides of Huancavelica and the town nestles within them as though enjoying the safety and security that they give. I try to find fancy words to describe my first view of Huancavelica, but in the end I have to say it is just beautiful.

There are many shoeshine boys on hand and for one sol (about 20p) my shoes are turned from being dusty and dirty to a gleaming advert for any new shoes. My next acquaintance is a captivating little girl of about eleven in a yellow and green football top; she

31

Huancavelica town and market

has jet-black hair and appears genuinely pleased to see us. She makes no effort to ask for money and her smile is charming. I ask if I can take her photograph and she is delighted; this photograph will probably be my everlasting memory of Huancavelica as it carried friendliness, pleasure, trust and interest; all things that I encountered in our all too short a stay in this town.

I give her one sol and she is even more delighted, and when we leave for our hotel she runs after the bus for a long time, waving madly to me. I get teased about this but it is both humbling and delightful to be able to give such pleasure.

An old man offers himself for a photo, but wants money first! He is easily persuaded to proceed the other way round. A local tells me that the old man scrapes a living by doing odd delivery jobs for people and that one sol for him would be a lot of money. He is very self-conscious on the first photograph but has a real smile on the second.

My hotel is the Presidente, and is situated on the main square. Two sides of the square are small shops, a few houses and two Internet cafés. There is a row of cloisters on the third, and our hotel and the cathedral makes up the other. In the centre there is a nice paved area with seats, trees and small gardens.

The whole scene is dominated by a towering mountain and is quite delightful.

After checking in, I decide to explore and soon find that not all the streets are quite so well looked after, as many of them are very uneven with lots of potholes. The only vehicles appear to be the odd pickup truck and taxis. I am looking for a souvenir and find some outdoor stalls where they seem to sell everything you can think of in alpaca, wool or fibres. I opt for a nice beige alpaca scarf and manage to haggle two soles off the price; this is more for the challenge of doing it rather than trying to save money.

Later, I find an absolute labyrinth of a market (mostly indoor) that seems to sell just about everything you could think of, even a skinned cow's head, complete with horns and eyes that have a definite baleful look. It has been sitting on the floor in the warmth of the sun and the smell follows me for some time afterwards. Even now some weeks later as I write up these notes, the memory makes me think that I can still smell it.

Next I buy a box *of mate de coca*. These are teabags made from the leaves of the coca plant, from which they derive cocaine. Coca tea is reputed to suppress one's appetite and supply energy. It is also good for combating altitude sickness and I have started to both drink it and chew the leaves, to good effect.

Nearly every meal that I have had so far in Peru has been preceded by a glass of Pisco Sour and because I have so taken to it I am looking for a bottle of the main ingredient. Pisco is a clear liquor to which is added the juice of a lemon, sugar, crushed ice and the white of an egg.

The mixture is gently shaken and served, and is one of the nicest drinks that I have ever tasted; it doesn't take many to have an effect either! Down a side street we find a room off the street (shop would be too grand a name) where a man is selling 96% liquor from large barrels; you bring your own jug and help yourself. I am very tempted but haven't got a jug. I buy a litre of Pisco and a litre of Cancun Ora; this is a golden coloured rum (ron), and it was the colour and worn state of the label as much as anything that persuaded me to buy it. I have yet to try the rum.

The whole transaction only cost me fifteen soles.

We are quite clearly the only Europeans visible in the town but everyone is very friendly towards us and will smile, wave or chat. The whole atmosphere of the town is inviting.

After dinner, which is taken at a local restaurant, I return to the hotel as I plan another early night, despite the fact that we have a late start in the morning – nine o'clock!

The hotel has a slightly colonial air with interior and fittings to match but is nevertheless very comfortable. Breakfast the following morning is excellent: eggs, fresh fruit juice, fresh bread, jam, fresh fruit and strong coffee. Plenty of everything, and I feel set up for the day.

Huancavelica is the end of the Central Railroad and today we are travelling 220 miles by road to Ayacucho, where we will stay the night before flying to Cuzco to continue our journey, this time on the Southern Railroad.

We have a smart fifty-seater coach for our eight-hour journey to Ayacucho, and as we wait to start a group of young men in matching tracksuits come marching past in quick time. I am not sure whether they are some form of militia, but they certainly don't show any signs of fatigue, despite the altitude. As we pull out of town we pass some street vendors at the side of the road who are selling their goods from three-wheeled bicycles.

The two wheels are at the front and carry a wooden slatted tray about three foot square on which the goods are carried and displayed.

It had been intended that the line from Huancavelica would continue to the coast, and during World War II construction of the bridges and embankments from Huancavelica as far as Lachoc were actually completed, but rails were not laid. The project was then abandoned at the end of the war.

Very soon we are climbing quite steeply and the road is climbing the mountain in a double S-bend. Halfway up, and we can see one of the bridges on the unused section of the former line. Sixty years on and it still looks in good condition with its massive stone abutments.

Soaring mountains surround us, and although the view between them and us is somewhat bleak it is still very impressive thanks to the sheer scale of everything. Occasionally we pass a small mud-walled dwelling with a woven grass roof and a mud-walled compound for the animals. These are usually in an area where there is nothing else as far as the eye can see, and to my mind it suggests a very basic existence. Occasionally there are little pieces of cultivation to be seen on the side of the mountain, despite the fact that the ground is almost vertical.

The road at this point is quite hair-raising, with a cliff on one side and a sheer drop on the other, and our large fifty-seater coach seems quite inappropriate for this type of road, even if it wasn't being driven at what appears to be a breakneck speed... We've just gone over a section where the road has been washed away by some previous torrent coming down from the mountain, and it hasn't occurred to the driver to slow down.

We are now in a broad valley with lots of rough grass, and the mountains are quite breathtaking with their constantly changing colours, which at the moment are white, gold, brown, grey and ochre; a colour spectacular.

We have just seen many llamas, maybe 200 to 300, and have made a photo stop. The llamas decide to keep their distance, and a photo may not be much use, but it is nice to see them in their natural environment, unlike those at Machu Picchu, which have been 'imported' to please the tourists. In the distance there is a small town called Astrobamba; it is a very poor town and the people make their living selling the wool of the llamas, from which they make about $50 a month.

It is very high at this point and we are advised to walk slowly and it seems to take me an age to walk from one side of the road to the other, Even so, I can feel the effects of the altitude.

We have made another brief stop, this time at a road junction. The significance of this location is that it is the highest point that we will reach on any part of our journey through Peru. Here we are at 16,400 feet above sea level, or as I expressed it at the time, half as high as the airliners fly. I decide not to expend any energy here other than taking a photograph of the road sign, which reads:

Huancayo 55 km
Huancavelica 202 km
Minacaubalosa 20 km
Huachocolpa 33 km

16,400 feet above sea level (more than 3 miles!)

We are now in an area that was virtually a no-go area in the 1980s and early 1990s because of a revolutionary group called Sendero Luminoso (Shining Path), who pursued a guerrilla war against the government during that time.

Ten minutes later and we are passing an incredibly blue lake that we are told is very deep. It is also the water source for Pisco, a city on the coast halfway between San Juan and Lima.

We have come across a shepherd and five alpacas at the roadside. There is no sign of habitation as far as the eye can see but he apparently comes from a village called Chocacocha. This village was at the edge of yet another lake, but had to be rebuilt further up the shore because the other village was under water when the mountain snow melted and raised the water level. The alpacas are white and very endearing, and it is something of a shock to learn that the shepherd is on his

What are you staring at!

way to sell them to the slaughterhouse. He says that he will get about eighty soles for each one.

There is much demand for photographs, and our driver subjects the shepherd to a torrent of Spanish. It turns out that he is telling the shepherd to take off his 'Pepsi' peaked cap and put on a traditional 'pixie'-style hat.

This is an area where there are pumas, but our guide says that they are not often seen.

After driving through miles and miles of vast plain with nothing but sparse grass we start to climb a hill at the side of another large lake. I can just see a small rowing boat at the water's edge.

At the top there is a small town where we are scheduled to stop for lunch. The town is called Santa Iñes, and in addition to a church and school there are many houses, most of which line the dusty and wide main road that cuts through the middle of the town.

We stop outside Restaurant el Favorito, a long low building with a corrugated iron roof. We are welcome to look at the kitchen,

Santa Ines Main Street

and everything in it has obviously been used many times. There are large galvanised pots sitting on top of ancient gas cookers. The floor is of beaten earth and the walls are lined with blue polythene; there is also a post in the middle that seems to play a part in keeping the roof up.

The lady in charge speaks no English but is very welcoming and obviously proud of her establishment. At a bench in the corner two locals and our driver are enjoying a meal.

Stuart says that he can recommend the food and I decide to forgo the packed lunch in favour of *trucha*. This is a trout that was caught only an hour ago and it is fried and served with rice, cucumber, onions and potatoes. I also have a cup of real coca tea -that is to say, the cup is packed with the actual leaves rather that the usual teabag. The trout is beautifully cooked with not a bone in sight. In addition, the skin is a perfection of crispness and delicious to eat. The whole meal is one of the best that I have ever tasted and the total bill is a mere five soles.

Some of us sit and chat with locals outside their house; everyone here is very friendly and welcoming. The remoteness and primitive-ness of this town I find very appealing and attractive. I can only imagine that whatever the hardships, life in this town is probably very simple and straightforward, and one of my favourite photographs from Peru is the view of the dusty main street of Santa Iñes.

We leave at about a quarter to one, and half an hour later pass through a village called Pilpichaca. It is a very ramshackle-looking place and I have only noted it because of the solar-powered public phone box by the side of the road.

Ten minutes later and the road surface suddenly becomes tarmac; we have been four and a half hours on dirt track roads.

As we drop down from the Rumichaca Pass (12,795 feet) we enter an area where a particular type of cactus called Poyara-munde grows. Because of the climate and soil at this point, it is the only area of Peru that it is found in. Sadly, the single specimen that we can see appears to have been the victim of a bush fire; nevertheless it is still impressive and it looks like a 30-foot black torpedo stood on its end.

We are driving through an area called Muchac. This used to be a very volcanic area and we can see an enormous large mound of what looks like solidified streams of yellow, black, white, and grey water; it is in fact a volcanic overflow from those times.

We have climbed to 15,400 feet and as we drop down towards Ayacucho we reach the village of Icapa. There is a market in progress and we make a short stop. This is obviously a very poor area and it is reflected in the items for sale, which are mostly rather tired-looking fruit and vegetables, together with some hats, scarves and ponchos. Our arrival causes quite a stir and it is obvious that Europeans are rarely, if ever, seen here. Everybody is very friendly and this is something that we found throughout Peru. Perhaps against his better judgement, I persuade Joseph, my companion, to buy a Stetson. I have to say that I thought it suited him, but it is still one of those things that you buy on holiday and then wonder what to do with it when you get home.

Icapa Market

There are now lots of trees and a river and the road winds up and around with many S-bends but finally after 8 hours we arrive in Ayacucho.

This is where the Shining Path (Sendero Luminoso) was founded and flourished, and their leader was Abimael Guzman. He was a Professor of Philosophy at the local university and believed that the only way to mount a revolution was through violence. During their guerrilla war against the Peruvian government in the 1980s and 1990s, there were over 30,000 deaths; but following the election of Alberto Fujimori to president in 1990, a tough line was taken against the Shining Path, and this resulted in the arrest, trial and imprisonment of Guzman in 1992.

Our hotel is in a side street just off the main square and is a large and impressive building, particularly when you get inside. Again, there is a colonial feel to the place, with its terrazzo-floored foyer and enclosed gardens. My room has a somewhat dated air about it but it is very comfortable and well equipped, with soap, shoe-cleaning equipment, towels and all the other needs of a traveller.

After eight hours on the coach I am ready for bed, but I am also aware that we have an extremely early start in the morning to catch our plane to Cuzco, and tonight will probably be the only opportunity to see something of the town.

Outside the hotel there is a lot of noise and activity, and when I venture out, I find myself on the edge of a mass of humanity that fills the street from side to side; it is obviously a celebration or festival of some kind, as there are many brightly-coloured costumes and floats. Although there are many adults following the procession, the floats and costumes are occupied by boys and girls aged between about eight and eleven. There are also many young women of about eighteen to twenty involved in the procession. It is a shame that I was not able to find out what the celebration was all about, although I did discover that there are many beautiful young women in Ayacucho.

The atmosphere is one of pure enjoyment and I can't resist joining the procession behind the floats. Despite the fact that I am the only foreigner I am made welcome by several people, although the contact puts a severe strain on my limited Spanish.

The procession wends its way to the main square, which is mostly cobbled and is surrounded by very attractive sixteenth and seventeenth-century Spanish-style buildings. There are cloisters on one side with many brightly-coloured shops beneath their arches, and everywhere there is noise, gaiety and music; everyone is undoubtedly having a wonderful time.

I stick with the procession for about an hour while it wends its way along narrow streets, gathering more people on the way, until finally I decide that in view of our early start I had better head for bed. It has been a most exhilarating experience.

I sleep well that night despite the altitude and am up, washed and dressed by 5 a.m.

Breakfast in the morning is a slow affair; perhaps 5.15 a.m. is a bit early for our group, but we are due to leave by six o'clock. I must get at least a couple of photographs before we leave, and not far from the hotel is San Cristobal, which is the Ayacuchans' first church. There are many churches in Ayacucho, including Santa Teresa, with its ornate fountain under the shade of a beautiful tree, and the Church of El Arco with its monument of a local heroine, Maria Parado de Bellido.

The main square at six in the morning is very attractive (and quite different from last night), and deserted except for one solitary walker. The paved walkways and gardens are spotlessly clean and tidy. Were there really thousands of people here last night?

Ayacucho at dawn

The gardens are full of attractive flowers and there is a jacaranda in full bloom. A subdued glow spreads over the whole square as the sun inches its way up in an attempt to clear the church at the far side of the square. A shaft of sunlight finds a way through via a side street. The whole scene is incredibly peaceful and beautiful.

Our transfer to Ayacucho Airport is swift and uneventful. On arrival, I avail myself of the services of the ubiquitous shoeshine boy. The passport formalities are soon dealt with and we have a few minutes to wait before boarding our plane.

The departure 'lounge' is devoid of anything except a few chairs, but I suppose people are not kept waiting long enough to need other facilities and so it proves.

Our sleek white plane, marked in the blue and yellow of Aero Continente, awaits us on the tarmac for the ninety-minute flight to Lima. Our next scheduled stop after Ayacucho is actually Cuzco, but we cannot fly direct and have to go via Lima.

The plane is a Fokker F28, and although considerably smaller than those that I am used to, it is the nicest plane that I have travelled on. The seats are very comfortable and there is plenty of legroom. We even have refreshments served, and the journey time passes very quickly. We arrive at Lima just after 9 a.m.

Our plane from Lima to Cuzco is a Boeing 727 and we leave just after 10 a.m. The legroom on this plane is so restricted that I don't think I can actually get into my seat!

I am saved by being offered a seat next to the emergency exit.

Cuzco: after Manco Capac, son of the Sun God, and Mama Occlo, daughter of the Moon, rose from the waters of Lake Titicaca, they began a journey looking for a place to settle, and their travels brought them to a spot where Manco Capac plunged his golden staff into the ground, only for it to sink and disappear from sight. They called this spot Cuzco, the navel of the earth, and it eventually became the capital of the Inca Empire.

I should have been prepared, but Cuzco comes as somewhat of a shock. The arrivals hall is a heaving mass of tourist humanity, and they are being entertained by a group of musicians dressed in traditional costumes. There are information booths, porters and guides, all offering their services. This is the eye of the needle through which mass tourism threads its way on the road to Machu Picchu, and I find it a slightly depressing experience after travelling through so many places untouched by tourism. It is, I suppose, a slightly selfish view, as Machu Picchu is undoubtedly the main tourist attraction of South America, and as such brings in a lot of much-needed currency. There are nevertheless, many beautiful things to see and do in Cusco.

The transfer to the hotel is uneventful and I arrive there at about noon. It is very hot, and although the altitude in Cusco is 11,000 feet, I am feeling no ill effects.

Cusco is saturated with tourists, but our tour takes in many narrow streets and it is amazing to see all the Inca foundations on many of the buildings.

Our tour guide is Juan Cornejo. He is a knowledgeable guide with a true love of his country and its traditions and music. He is enthusiastic about the traditional language of the Incas, Quechua. This is still spoken by many people in Peru, including Juan, and is an official language alongside Spanish.

Juan is also an accomplished musician, and later in the trip I buy a CD of Traditional Cusco music performed by him and Raul Bohorquez. The title of the CD is Urpillay (Sweetheart) and I am playing it as I write up these notes.

Our city tour takes in the Plaza de Armas, the Cathedral, La Piedra de Los Doce Angulos. We also visit the Sun Temple of Koricancha, where there is much evidence of Inca stonework, and also the remains of three internal temples: The Stars, Thunder and Rain, and The Rainbow.

There is now just time to visit Sacsayhuaman before we return to our hotel and dinner.

Sacsayhuaman is a massive fortress and religious site high on a hill above Cusco.

Many of the stones that were used to construct Sacsayhuaman weighed over one hundred tons each; they all fit together with amazing precision. The sheer scale of the site is awesome, and the view from up here of Cusco in the valley far below, is quite spectacular.

Later we visit another Inca site close to Sacsayhuaman where we have the opportunity to view a sacrificial stone within a cave.

Cusco from Sacsayhuaman

Sacsayhuaman

It is quite a thought to stand there and visualise what happened on that massive stone many hundreds of years ago. There are two small children clutching lambs at the entrance and hoping for a sole or two in exchange for a photograph.

There is just time to make a 'tourist stop' at a shop selling traditional goods. I don't mind, as I am anxious to buy an alpaca rug for someone special back home. Prices in the shop are very high and haggling is hard work, but thanks to Stuart's support I end up with what I consider to be a bargain, so everyone is happy.

Outside the shop there is a white llama standing with a very bored expression on its face. It has obviously seen many tourists before and quite clearly finds nothing new or special in me. It seems very approachable and I stroke the soft fur along its back until, quite suddenly, it quickly turns and spits in my face. The llama's aim is very accurate.

After a wash and change at our hotel we are off to Jose Antonio's restaurant for dinner and a floor show. The restaurant is fairly full when we arrive and it is a very cosmopolitan gathering. The selection of food is mouth-watering and I have, in turn, alpaca, *cuy* (guinea pig), and *ceviche*, preceded by the ever-present pisco.

The floor show is also excellent with a group of young people, sometimes in traditional dress singing traditional Inca songs and sometimes in costumes in which they dance and re-enact stories and tales from the past. It is fast, frenetic and very enjoyable; a very satisfying end to the day.

A slight problem with the altitude during the night but nothing as bad as that at Huancayo.

Another early start in the morning and we are at Cusco Station next to the colonial church of San Pedro. There is a smartly dressed attendant allocated to each coach for the journey, and our attendant is called Indira. The train leaves spot on time at 6 a.m. for the three-and-a-half-hour journey.

The climb out of Cusco is so steep that the train has to zigzag up it. This involves travelling up a gradient, waiting, changing

46

points and then travelling up another gradient in the opposite direction. This process is then repeated until we are at the summit. As we climb, the view of Cusco becomes an attractive sea of red and brown roofs, but here there is plenty of evidence of poverty too, with poor mud brick houses and rubbish on both sides of the line.

As we reach the summit of our climb (12,000 feet) we leave the houses behind and the view is now of many smallholdings where they are engaged in the making of mud bricks for houses. These are cut squares of mud with straw or grass which are then left in the sun to dry and harden.

At about eleven kilometres from Cusco we reach what is a brand new station called Poroy. The intention is that passengers will soon be bussed from Cusco to this station, thereby avoiding the long slow climb out of Cusco by rail; the more cynical might think that it is to avoid the paying customers seeing the poverty of the people that live on the mountainside.

At Poroy we can see the Hiram Bingham Train. This is a brand new train due to go into service for the first time next week. The carriages are all very luxurious and are fitted out in 'Orient Express' style.

We are now passing through a very fertile and agricultural valley and there are lots of yellow flowers, very green willow trees and various crops. This area is known as the 'Breadbasket of Cusco' and virtually all the food for the town comes from this area.

It's 7.10 a.m. and we have just passed Iscuchaca Station, and as we cross the road and continue to follow the Rio Huarcondo we start to turn away from the valley area and enter a gorge where there are lots of eucalyptus trees. There is a station here with the same name as the river, Huarcondo. While the gorge is not as imposing as that which we travelled through on the way to Huancavelica, the backdrop of very high mountains still give it an impressive feel. By 8 a.m., we are now back in the valley. This very fertile valley runs from east to west and has its own enclosed climate with twelve hours' day and twelve hours' night.

We have just crossed the river at Paccar and I can see a lot of restored Inca terracing on the far side of the river, where they used to farm their crops. The Urubamba Mountains are shrouded in cloud and mist, and as we pass Ollantaytambo I can see lots of cactuses here, and later with beautiful pale and bright yellow flowers.

Lineside market

Ollantaytambo is the scene of a rare Inca victory against the Spanish in 1536, and the massive stone terraces from which the victory against the conquistadors was achieved are still there.

Just past Ollantaytambo, and we are now forty-two miles from Cuzco. The road to Quillabamba has now turned away to the right. From this point, the railway is the only way into Machu Picchu, and the cliffs are now towering above us on the right-hand side. It has been raining for the last half-hour and we have just passed an Inca bridge over the river.

We have passed through a fairly long tunnel and we are now in a spectacular gorge with the river tumbling alongside us. This

The Inca Bridge

area is semi-tropical and there are lots of trees; here it is cloudy for eight months of the year.

The area is called Pampacahua and there is a station of the same name.

Suddenly, there is an extraordinary sight. At the line side there are some men working with a JCB, and on the side of the JCB is the word 'Jarvis'. It seems incredible to travel 7,000 miles to find a Jarvis JCB in a Peruvian jungle!

It is 9.30 a.m. and we are quite close to Machu Picchu station. I can see amaryllis growing wild at the side of the railway, a wonderful sight. At Machu Picchu Station we all get off and transfer to a single diesel unit for the final leg to the hydroelectric station.

It is now very tropical and brightly-coloured cockatiels dart among the trees. All around are shrubs and greenery coming down to the water's edge. There is a lot of water in the river and it is rushing headlong over huge boulders worn smooth by many years of attritional treatment. The mountains are shrouded in mist. There

Machu Picchu Station   The way back

are bananas, passion fruit and avocados growing alongside the railway, but it is hard to tell whether they are cultivated or growing wild. The sensation of the train heading into a jungle is very real at this point and we almost seem like invaders of another world.

The railway is twisting and turning as it follows the river and at one point we cross it, only to cross back again. Not long afterwards and we have reached the hydroelectric plant. The line literally runs through the middle of the plant, and it is at that point that our journey is ended. The line originally ran through for another fifteen miles to Quillabamba but was closed five years ago following a landslip. As we descend from the train I can see that the line finishes at the mouth of a rock tunnel some fifty metres further on; the tunnel has been blocked up, as the landslip was just beyond the mountain through which the tunnel passed. It seems a shame that Quillabamba has been deprived of its railway service after so many years. It has a population of about 25,000, and various crops are grown there both for local consumption and markets beyond. From my probably ignorant point of view, I would have thought that there was enough cheap local labour to rebuild the severed line.

The manager of the plant is very welcoming and we are to have a complete tour, including the vast underground cavern where the turbines are situated.

Even the guard with the pump-action shotgun seems welcoming. The water for the turbines is extracted from the local river and then fed into pipes at a point 500 feet above the plant. At the top there is a maintenance and inspection point, and this is reached from ground level by an almost vertical railway, up which is hauled, by cable, a wooden trolley with six bench seats. The view upwards is quite intimidating and I have to persuade myself that it really is safe by remembering that it is used every day by inspection teams. The ride up is very slow and really is almost vertical. One of our party keeps her head lowered all the time and does respond very well to comments such as, 'Look how far down it is!' and, 'Isn't this great?'

There is not much to see but we are taken to the point at which the water is forced down a narrow channel and into the pipes; the speed and power of it is quite frightening.

The view from the top is quite breathtaking, and our train far below looks like a little toy; sometimes it is possible to see part of Machu Picchu from here, but not today, because of the mist. For one tantalising moment part of it is revealed, but almost

The Hydroelectric Station

instantly covered again in mist, and the effect is to increase our sense of anticipation for the visit there tomorrow.

The ride down is more hair-rising as we now have our backs to the descent.

We have now entered the building where all the machinery is located and the noise is deafening; our guide does not seem to notice and carries on explaining things to us. There is a lift that takes us down to the vast underground cavern where the turbines are situated, and apart from some maintenance work, the area is spotless. One wall is taken up with a huge mural depicting Inca folklore.

It has been drizzling all through our visit and the rain steadily increases as we return to our train. We're back in Machu Picchu Station about 12.30 and have lunch at a local restaurant. It is now pouring down.

The restaurant is full and obviously very popular, but although the food is very nice I find the choice somewhat limited. The view from where I am sitting is of the river, swollen by rain, tumbling and crashing over huge boulders as it makes its way down the valley. The greenery, the river and the mist-shrouded mountains give the whole scene an almost primeval air.

The railway runs straight through the middle of this small town and there are shops, restaurants and market stalls crowding in on both sides of the track. Even with the rain there are a lot of people about, looking for souvenirs, food or just somewhere to shelter from the rain.

It is 4 p.m. and still teeming down with rain. Stuart says that it never rains two days running here; I am not sure whether this is true or just meant to cheer us up for tomorrow, when we are to visit the sanctuary of Machu Picchu. I am really looking forward to it, rain or no rain.

The Machu Picchu Pueblo Hotel where we are staying is a short walk from the station and is a series of log cabins built into the jungle. They are well appointed and very comfortable. Outside it is difficult to see what is cultivated and what is natural jungle, but the whole effect is of wildness and is very pleasing. As I walk down to the building that houses the lounge and restaurant, the noises of the night are both familiar and strange but also soothing.

The lounge oozes comfort, with large settees and a huge open fireplace with a log fire burning. The dinner and company are both excellent.

As I later make my way back to my cabin I reflect that being in this tropical area is an exhilarating experience, although I must confess to looking both under and in my bed before getting into it. Urban dwellers...!

I fall asleep to the night sounds and the crashing of the river that is just outside my window.

In the morning there is a heightened sense of anticipation: this is the day that we visit Machu Picchu. I have seen many pictures of it but never thought that I would one day actually stand and look at it.

After breakfast, we cross the railway and walk to the bottom of the hill that runs through this small town to catch a bus. Even though it is only 6.30 it is already busy with the traders' stalls alongside the railway set up and doing business. There is a gang of workers putting in a new pedestrian crossing in the railway, and part of the dirt roadway to where the buses are parked has now been paved, no doubt as a result of demand from the more well-heeled tourists.

The journey to Machu Picchu will take about fifteen minutes and the driver seems keen to set some sort of new record, as he negotiates the backward and forward zigzags up the mountain over the narrow dirt track road at an alarming speed. There is very little concession to a reduction in speed, even when we meet a coach coming down. This dirt track road is known as the Hiram

Bingham Highway after the man who discovered Machu Picchu in 1911, and it ends outside the Sanctuary Lodge Hotel.

On a raised bank there is a large diagram of the ruins, and Juan gathers us round this very much like a sheepdog gathering in sheep. With his theatrical stance and baton, he is very much like one of his Inca ancestors addressing the people.

The main entrance to the sanctuary is directly off the car park, but Juan has other ideas and leads us on a tortuous climb that seems to be taking us away from the site. I should have given him more credit, for he has brought us to a high point overlooking the city of Machu Picchu.

Machu Picchu   Ambition fulfilled

Nothing really prepares you for Machu Picchu. I have seen so many images of it, and although it has always been a place of great interest for me it has also been somewhere far away. Juan had previously described Machu Picchu as having a power and an

What a setting   Though the arch   Stairs

Orchids at Machu Pichu   Intihuatana

aura, but I had merely put this down to his overenthusiastic manner
and flowery speech.

In fact, this place has serenity and magic all rolled into one.
Perched high above, I look down on the houses, temples and
agricultural terraces that were home to many people hundreds of
years ago, and the scene gives me a sense of calm.

Machu Picchu is built on a promontory. Hundreds of feet below,
the Urubamba River winds its way around the base, but up here
it is another world. It is very quiet and there are few visitors about
as we make our way down to the point from which the most
publicised photograph of Machu Picchu is taken. There is a group
photograph, and also one of myself, taken against the backdrop
of Huayna Picchu, the 'Young Peak' that towers at the corner of
the site. Three of our group later climb this peak. All around us
are towering tree-clad mountains shrouded in mist, and as I position
myself and look at the city and Huayna Picchu through the lens
of my camera I experience an almost orgasmic thrill and a tingle
runs through my body. Even now when I tell people about Machu
Picchu I experience that same feeling.

To the west there are rows of houses leading down to the Sun
Temple. This temple was of major importance for the Incas, who,
in addition to believing that plants and natural phenomena had
living souls, also believed that the mountains were gods, with the
Sun being the greatest god of all.

On this side of the site is the sacred rock of this Inca city and
it is called Intihuatana. It is a sundial, and its four corners are

aligned not only with the cardinal points but also with four sacred peaks in the surrounding mountains. The stone would also have indicated when crops should be planted and was probably the most important site in the city. These stones are very rare in Peru, as the Spanish tried to destroy everything that was connected with what they saw as pagan sun worship.

Behind me I can see the remains of the quarry where the stones of Machu Picchu came from. The scale of this place is breathtaking, with dizzying heights or vertigo-inducing drops, and in the middle of this, a perfectly positioned and proportioned city. As we walk down a winding track alongside banks of houses we reach the Sun Temple and one of the very few two-storey dwellings, probably built for a princess.

There is a long and steep stone staircase looking as good now as when it was built. The system whereby water was carried to all levels of the city is still in place, and water gurgles and sparkles in it today.

On the top of a peak high above the city, some intrepid soul has planted the Inca flag and it flutters proudly in the breeze

Machu Picchu is a place where you drink in the surroundings like a parched man would drink water, but eventually it is time to move on for lunch at the nearby hotel. While I am there I get a conducted tour of the hotel and get roped in as an 'actor', posing as guest being introduced to the facilities of the hotel, it is all part of a promotion video for Stuart's company.

Back at Aguas Calientes there is time to wander among the many stalls that crowd in on each side of the railway line. Crafts and souvenirs, films, dolls, ponchos, cafés, restaurants, walking sticks, umbrellas, drinks and sweets ... the list is almost endless. Things here are dearer than I have seen them elsewhere, but who can blame the traders? They will drop the price quite sharply if you start to walk away.

Our train leaves at 3.30 p.m. for the three-and-a-half-hour trip to Cusco, and the next stage of our journey.

Everyone is pretty relaxed after what has been a long, busy and

Market day at Machu Picchu

fulfilling day, but later in the journey this mood is quickly changed as one of the train attendants appears. He is dressed in a brightly-coloured costume with a head mask of what appears to be an extremely aggressive sheep, or it might be a wolf. He is carrying a stick with coloured ribbons on the end and he performs an aggressive and threatening dance from one end of the carriage to the other; the significance of the dance is not explained but we are treated to an encore. The other two attendants then put on a fashion show; it is obviously a prelude to selling the items, but is still very enjoyable.

It is hard to believe that the girl works as a railway attendant and not in a fashion shop as, with her flowing hair, sparkling eyes, eye-catching figure and genuine smile, she parades the various changes up and down the carriage as though she was born to it.

The rest of the journey passes uneventfully until we reach the top of the mountain above Cusco. It is now quite dark, and as we descend, the city below us is a mass of thousands of twinkling lights.

At the station our coach is waiting to take us to our hotel. The organisation on this trip has been extremely efficient so far and obviously reflects considerable work behind the scenes.

Had a bad night's sleep; the room seemed very hot and airless but I got by without oxygen. I think it was the result of the recent altitude changes, for in the last three days we have gone from 16,000 feet to sea level, to 11,000 feet, to 8,000 feet and back to 11,000 feet. I am probably tired as well.

We are making yet another early start in the morning for the eight o'clock train to Puno and our hotel at the side of Lake Titicaca. It's a ten-hour journey.

Estación Cuzco is next to the colonial church of San Pedro and is a modern blue and cream building with rows of sightless windows. I realise that I have left my jacket in the hotel but this is no problem as the taxi driver volunteers to fetch it for me.

The people of Peru are so friendly and helpful.

There is a long line of blue carriages with a yellow stripe along the side and at the front, a large diesel locomotive in matching livery. Each coach has a personal attendant waiting to greet you as you board. Ours is an attractive girl called Indira and she will be with us for the 384-kilometre journey to Puno and later to Arequipa, Mollendo and return to Arequipa.

It would be easy to say that the journey through the suburbs of Cusco is without interest, but everything about this country is interesting – perhaps sometimes featureless, but always changing. We have just passed a very tall stone monument with the figure of a long dead hero on the top. We are now passing through the very fertile Urubamba Valley and on top of a hill in the distance I can see a huge statue of Christ, it is the same one that we were able to see from Sacsayhuaman a few days ago. There are a lot of eucalyptus trees.

Once you get outside the urban area, the level of existence appears very basic, and I can see a group of six or seven people following two oxen that are pulling a piece of wood through the ground. Considering the vastness of the valley and the lack of any obvious boundaries, the tilling of the ground appears to be a project that puts the painting of the Forth Bridge into shade.

Close to the railway is someone making mud bricks by the simple expedient of cutting out turfs about one foot square by six inches deep and then leaving them in the sun to dry. It seems to me to be a very efficient housing strategy, for if you have to move on, then you simply leave your dwelling to the elements and construct a new one elsewhere, with the only cost being your own labour.

The carriages are very luxurious. They are copies of an Orient Express carriage, from the opulent days, but were actually made in Cusco two years ago. There are tablecloths, table lights, flowers and all the seating is individual armchairs. There is much wood panelling and gleaming brass work, and all the staff, attendants and chefs are immaculately turned out.

There is also on-board entertainment with a man playing what looks like a guitar, but probably isn't, and he is accompanied by a woman who is encouraging people to perform a national dance with her.

Dancing on the train

Their costumes are very highly coloured, and an integral part is a hat that looks like a round table mat with a long red frilly tassel all around it. After a little persuasion I attempt a few steps but the difference in our respective heights makes the movements somewhat difficult, not to mention comical. I am not sure that me wearing the hat does anything serious for the spectacle, either.

The view at the moment is blue sky with fluffy white clouds and a seemingly never-ending line of mountains.

The vastness of the plain continues and we are just passing a woman standing in the middle of a field leaning on a spade. She is wearing a red skirt, blue top and a wide-brimmed black hat; but the most interesting part of the scene is that there is no sign of another person or dwelling as far as the eye can see. This has been a typical view for the last three hours.

We have reached Sicuani (11,620 feet) and are now 140 kilometres from Cusco. This is a quite a big town with paved roads and street lights, although the main form of transport appears to be three-wheeled bikes with an attached seating compartment.

There is a large market with stalls literally right up to the railway track; they even use the space between the sleepers once the train has passed. There are a lot of sidings and derelict sheds here.

Ever since we left Cusco we have been following a major river called Vilcanota, but not long after we leave Sicuani it dwindles in size and importance; this is about the point at which we pass the town of Chectuyoc. Here I can see an extremely elegant mansion and church; they are very different from the rest of the town buildings and have tiled roofs and glassed windows, very striking amongst the usual mud-walled houses.

As we near Aguas Calientes some six miles further on, we pass through what seems like a tropical storm, although this area is not tropical. There are huge hailstones and within moments the ground is white. Amazingly, some two miles further on at Aguas Calientes, there is a little girl bathing in a hot spring at the side of the railway with no sign of hailstones anywhere.

We have now reached La Raya. This is the highest point (14,500 feet) on the route to Puno and there is a scheduled stop here of about fifteen minutes, although there is no actual station as such and no passengers join or leave the train at this point. There is, however, a market in full swing and it is obviously a tourist stop for both road and rail traffic to buy souvenirs and for people to take photographs of the surrounding mountains, some of which are still snow-capped. The mountains, as always, are very impressive and rise sheer and black on all sides, with the foothills being a rich gold colour. The market is quite busy and there are all manner of things made with alpaca wool. I nearly buy a white hat with bobbles, which is quite beautiful, until I wonder when I would wear it at home.

La Raya

We have lunch on the train and it is quite delicious: avocado and red cabbage salad with warm freshly baked rolls, and a main course of beef tournedos with a dessert of *mousse de chirimoya*. This is mainly custard apple, heavy cream and passion fruit juice and is quite superb.

Eight hours on the train, and for the last two hours we have been passing through a vast dry plain with, very occasionally, a single dwelling in the distance. A few minutes later and we are now running through Juliaca. This is a large industrial town and as the train passes through the station I can see a steam locomotive parked in a siding, apparently abandoned. There are apparently endless stalls at the side of the railway track and it seems as though you can buy virtually anything, and even get your hair cut within three feet of the passing train.

We don't actually get as far as Puno Station, for the train has pulled up on a level crossing a mile or so from the town. The hotel is just a short walk from here and is the very new and very opulent-looking five-star Libertador Isla Esteves.

By the time I have checked in and had dinner it is too late to think about anything except bed. A bad night. We're at 12,500 feet and I am finding it impossible to get to sleep. Every time I close my eyes I get a feeling of claustrophobia. One complete wall of the bedroom is a huge window looking out on Lake Titicaca, and I open it wide. The cool breeze feels lovely and you can almost believe that there is plenty of oxygen in it, but there isn't.

I eventually give in about 3 a.m. and go in search of oxygen. The receptionist is very pleasant and understanding and takes me to a room where there is a bed with a huge green oxygen cylinder by the side of it. She puts a mask over my face and murmurs, 'Ten minutes, senor.' Within seconds of her closing the door I am fast asleep until I feel her gently shaking my shoulder and whispering, 'Half an hour, senor.' I feel amazingly refreshed, as though I had slept for hours.

Today is another highlight day, for we are headed for the floating islands of Lake Titicaca where the Uros Indians live.

From my bedroom window I can see Puno across the bay, shimmering in the haze, and outside the sun blazes down from a cloudless sky making the brilliant white of the hotel too dazzling to look at.

Lake Titicaca from my bedroom window

A motor launch is waiting, and from the back of the boat as we head out to the islands the hotel looks like the top half of a cruise liner hiding behind an island. Somehow the view does not jar and the building sits in a dip in the land as though it belonged there.

The islands are a wonderful sight. They are made from the Totora reeds that grow in Lake Titicaca and the pale gold of the islands and the deep blue of the water makes for some beautiful colour photographs. Their boats are made from the same reeds and have a slightly Viking appearance.

Although each island houses its own little community they are part of a whole, and there are about ten individual islands, each with about fifteen small reed and timber houses. One of the larger islands even has a small school on it, and children from the other islands are ferried to it each day.

We are invited to land, and the experience of walking on a floating island, made only from reeds, is quite strange – a bit like walking on a waterbed until you get used to it. The people are very welcoming and as they land, each guest is given a miniature replica of one of their boats, made from reeds. I later meet the man that makes these and he turns out to be the leader of the community. They also show us how they live and work on the island, including building a fire on a reed island to cook freshly-caught fish on hot stones. Many of the people are making blankets, shawls, hats and other items to sell to tourists; it seems that this is now their main source of income.

Tourists or not, they make us very welcome, and I am invited into the house of one of them. It is made of reeds and bamboo with many brightly-coloured rugs on the floor and washing hanging from a corner of the room. It is incredibly hot and the air is thick with flies, and as we pose together on the floor for a photograph, I wonder if they will turn out on the picture. Everywhere you look there is someone doing something: fishing, grinding corn, making trinkets and clothes, cooking, and even a little boy terrorising everyone with a football.

School on Lake Titicaca

Cooking on Lake Titicaca

Boat of reeds on Lake Titicaca

Home sweet home

It is time to visit another island, and the braver members of our party (including me) have volunteered to be ferried on one of their reed boats while the less intrepid take the launch. The woman who is going to ferry us across is only twenty-four but she makes light work of the half mile or so that separates us from the next island.

On this island there is an infant school and we are invited in to the one room that is their class. There is a delightful bunch of little children whose ages range from about four to about eight. Their attitude towards us includes curiosity, delight, amazement and even disinterest. One of my favourite photographs from Peru is one with a group of these children taken in their class.

The morning passes very quickly and we head across the bay to another hotel for lunch. As we tie up at the jetty we are almost alongside the Yavari. The Yavari was a British-built steamship that arrived in Arica (Chile, but formerly part of Peru) in 1862. The ship was, however, in 2,000 pieces and had to be carried to Lake Titicaca on pack mules, a feat that took six years; she was eventually

The Yavari

65

launched in 1870. Today she looks very smart in fresh black and white paint. The captain has promised to fire up the engines but we won't actually be leaving the dockside. The engines themselves are not the originals but are still quite old, 1913 four-cylinder Bolinder diesels. Everything below deck is gleaming brass and spotless. It seems a shame that after all the effort and smoke from the tunnel that we are not actually going to go anywhere.

I spend some time relaxing on the veranda of the nearby hotel, sipping pisco and drinking tea. It is incredibly relaxing to just sit in the sun watching the dark smoke from the funnel of the Yavari drifting over the blue waters of the lake and then into the cloudless sky. There is a sense of timelessness and peace here, and it is with a sense of reluctance that I eventually make a move. It is only a short walk back along the railway track to my hotel.

Last night was a repeat of the previous night; perhaps it is being by the lakeside or perhaps it is just brought on by tiredness.

A slightly later start today. The train for Arequipa leaves at 8 a.m. and we retrace our journey of two days ago as far as Juliaca.

Juliaca – Old and New

From here to Arequipa is 189 miles, and on that part of the journey we will pass Crucero Alto at 14,688 feet above sea level.

At Juliaca there is an opportunity for a photo stop and our train is positioned alongside the steam locomotive that I saw last time we passed. It doesn't look as though it gets steamed any more and just sits here as a reminder of a past era.

On our way out of Juliaca we pass hundreds of market stalls wedged between buildings and the railway track. They seem to go on and on. I suppose it was waiting to happen, but suddenly as we pass between them, with our siren blaring continually, the steps of our carriage demolish the stall of a woman selling vegetables. She herself appears unmoved but there is much hilarity among her fellow stallholders.

As I look out I can see that the steps are covered with leaves and when I investigate they turn out to be coca leaves, so I rescue an armful before they are blown away. All this is done while the train continues to sway along at about forty miles an hour. Imagine trying this on a train in the UK!

Pretty soon we are climbing to Crucero Alto. The view all around is now of scrubland and mountains; the desolate remoteness has a beauty all of its own. At 116 miles from Arequipa we make a short stop at Crucero Alto. There are extensive station buildings but no sign of any habitation; perhaps they all moved away when this part of Peru's rail system ceased to carry passengers. It is very hot and there is a sense of loneliness, our train being the only link with the outside world.

As we leave, we are only six miles from Chivay, a town on the edge of the Colca Canyon. In some places, this canyon is over two miles deep. This is home to the fabulous condors with their ten-foot wingspans that enable them to effortlessly ride the thermals.

Deep hills rise on each side of the Rio Colca that flows through the canyon. The agricultural terracing in these hills is over a thousand years old and still cultivated today.

We make another photo stop at Sumbay, where there is a deep gorge spanned by a wrought iron bridge. Not only do we have a

Sumbay

shot of our train on the bridge but also of all the staff on board who are looking after us. In the distance is the magnificent snow-capped Chanchi volcano.

A short stop at Pampa de Arrieros. We are now 174 miles from Puno, in another lonely spot with its station and buildings intact. Across the track from the station is an abandoned village. Despite its derelict air, I suddenly discover with a shock that it is inhabited. The straw roofs and mud walls look as though they would blow away in the first strong wind. How people survive up here is beyond me. There are a few goats but what they eat is a mystery as there is no sign of anything green as far as the eye can see. I can only admire the people who force a living out of this barren place. It is just a mountainous desert, but to my outside eye the place is beautiful.

We eventually arrive at Arequipa, which is Peru's second city, and transfer to the luxurious Hotel Libertador Arequipa.

Arequipa is also known as 'The White City' because of the many buildings constructed in ashlar, a white volcanic stone. The Plaza de Armas is both beautiful and busy; there is an attractive

Pampa de Arrieros

park in the centre that is surrounded by four lanes of traffic. There are colonnades round two sides and there are many buildings of interest, and just off the main square is the Santa Catalina Convent that dates from 1580. This is open to the public and the guided tour is like stepping back into Peru's past, with small plazas, beautiful courtyards and narrow streets. There is evidence everywhere of careful restoration, and with its delicately coloured walls, orange trees and potted plants it is a haven of peace and beauty. There are also some very beautiful landscapes around Arequipa, and from virtually every angle the city is dominated by the impressive volcanic cone of Misti.

There is time for a tour of Arequipa Station and the vast engineering workshops before we leave for the last leg of this rail journey, which, when finished, will have covered the entire rail system of Peru at a total distance of 1,044 miles.

Although Arequipa no longer serves passengers, the station is kept in immaculate order and the chocolate and cream frontage with its wrought ironwork and many doors and windows, looks

69

Arequipa Station

extremely attractive. The inside of the station is a copy of the
outside, except that it glistens in the hot sunlight. Across the station
garden I can see what I thought was a church but turns out to
be a private residence!

The station, tracks, sidings and engineering workshops cover a
vast area, which is not really surprising as Arequipa is the repair
centre for the entire rolling stock of the Southern Railroad.

The whole place is very quiet, and I learn that the huge numbers
of trains that used to carry soya and minerals have now dwindled
to a trickle, with a consequent drop in repair requirements. There
is an enormous twenty-track turntable surrounded by wagons of
various types, and all the other facilities, including the water tower
that existed for the servicing of steam locomotives, are still there.
The whole place seems timeless and it is deathly quiet.

At the back of one of the sheds and hidden behind an abandoned
coach there suddenly comes into view a little piece of history. On a
section of track overgrown with weeds is a 1918 Hunslet Saddle Tank
locomotive. It seems almost complete except for the driving rods. I

can imagine that any railway preservation group in England would be only too delighted to have such a locomotive and in such a condition. Behind it is another piece of history. This is a five-ton steam crane made by Jos Booth & Bros Ltd. of Leeds in 1927. The guide says that he had no idea they were here!

The cavernous workshops are also quiet with just three or four

A Hunslet at Arequipa

men working on some locomotives. Somebody has found time to make a miniature engineer out of bits of scrap metal, and he sits cheekily on top of a water valve.

Time to go. One hundred and twenty miles to Mollendo on the Pacific Coast.

As we leave the suburbs of Arequipa, the surrounding countryside becomes positively luxuriant, with many different crops and even palm trees. There is pre-Inca agricultural terracing still being cultivated today and I can see a lone figure hoeing in a field of crops. The intricate shapes and patterns of green fields, divided by low stone walls and hedges, stretch away to the horizon and

71

Inca terracing

the grey slopes of the slumbering volcanoes that surround Arequipa. Prickly-pear cactuses sit in orderly lines in the grey soil.

An eagle flies majestically past but too far away for a good photograph.

Tiabaya Station

Water means life

There is a short stop some eight miles from Arequipa at Tiabaya; already the scenery is changing, with just a few green trees among a vast expanse of grey and white desert. An abandoned water tower lies forlornly on its side in the dust. We had expected to allow a

Desert

freight train to pass at this point but it seems that the timings are wrong.

We are following the course of a river and for about 200 yards on each side of the river the ground is lush and cultivated.

The rest is grey and brown desert as far as the eye can see. It is a wonderful example of the fact that water means life.

We are now high in the mountains, miles from anywhere, and have made a short photo stop. The sun burns down from a cloudless sky and there is not a blade of anything green to be seen anywhere.

Later we pass a station literally in the middle of nowhere. The low yellow block building shimmers in the heat and, nearby, a water tower stands forlorn. It seems that the only function of this place, which I think is called Uchumayo, was for trains to pass and, in steam-hauled days, take on water.

The river that we followed earlier appears again, this time as a rushing torrent in a man-made concrete trough. A few miles further on, at Vitor, we find the reason. There is a substantial town here,

Uchumayo Station

with lots of buildings and green cultivation and also a lush football field where boys are playing a game, watched by a sizeable crowd. As I stand by the side of this three-feet-wide concrete trough with its rushing water, I reflect that it seems a very fragile link for this whole community to depend on. Just a short distance away is the desert waiting to claim back the land should the water stop flowing.

We have reached La Joya. From here the line used to carry straight on to Mollendo, but now it turns right for about thirty miles until it reaches a triangle just beyond Tintayani where the line splits. One way goes to the town of Mollendo and the other to the port of Matarani.

There is an eerie feel about La Joya. The abandoned station building still has a sign indicating that it is eighty-seven kilometres to Mollendo, the distance before the line was diverted. The water tower stands like some long-dead seven-legged monster. There is a dead feel about the place and it has become a graveyard for old coaches, wagons and oil tankers. In the distance there is a

La Joya

75

human graveyard with many ornate graves. Everywhere there is grey dust. An abandoned oil tanker stands forlornly pointing towards the coast as though waiting for some long-forgotten locomotive to help it complete its journey. With the hot dry atmosphere you can imagine that in fifty years' time these old wagons and tankers will still be sitting here in much the same condition.

On the way we pass some old and rusty oil tankers, victims of speed and sharp curves, left to rot. It reminds me how much our coach sways on some sections of the track. Best not to think about it.

Just a hole in the wall

We have reached the triangle and there is a very long train of tankers, hauled by three locomotives (in number order: 754, 755, 756!), waiting to continue its journey to Arequipa. It is an opportunity for photographs and some banter between the train crews.

* * *

Mollendo and the Pacific. Outwardly, Mollendo Station building is very attractive, with its wrought-iron and timber balcony set between two towers on stone plinths. Sadly, it is unlike any of the other stations that I have seen here, as inside it is quite dilapidated, and I take quite a risk to cross the timber floor to take a photograph from the balcony. Outside there are several rusty

Mollendo Station

and unused tracks occupied by equally rusty oil tankers. It is a scene of neglect. Mollendo as a railhead has obviously been long abandoned in favour of Matarani, as just beyond the station limit there are signs that many tracks used to extend alongside concrete jetties by the sea.

The town itself is quite busy and there are many stalls in the indoor market that I find. The sight of white Europeans is quite obviously a great novelty for the locals, and there are many stares. The fruit, vegetables and sweets are incredibly cheap.

As in every other place in Peru that I have visited, people are

Beach at Mollendo

very open and friendly and there is no sense of intimidation or discomfort.

The people of Mollendo have obviously made great efforts with their town and there are several very attractive squares with ornate

The Pacific

lighting and small gardens. The miles of sandy beach are a great attraction for many Peruvians, and they holiday here in great numbers in the season.

After a last look at the Pacific rollers, it is time to head back to the train for the return to Arequipa. We will have dinner on board, and with night fast approaching the two highlights of the return journey will be the sunset over the desert in about an hour's time and the thousand-mile mark as we pass San José.

The sunset is every bit as good as promised. As the sun sinks below the horizon, the sky above moves from yellow to gold to pale blue to rich dark blue. There are no clouds and the foreground is quite dark. Every eye on the train watches until the sun is gone.

As I write up these notes I am looking at the photographs that I took of the sunset and find two pictures ruined by light bars across them. At this point I had taken about 500 pictures without any problem. This was the last film and it was obviously faulty.

We could not see San José but there is much cheering as we pass through the station.

As we pass through the suburbs of Arequipa the tracks are in the highway, much like the fifties trams of Britain were. There is a lot of traffic about and nearly all of it travelling at great speed. There is now a situation with a line of fast-moving traffic alongside the fast-moving train, with a gap of about ten feet between. Suddenly a small car pulls out to overtake the line of traffic. He doesn't appear to realise that the traffic cannot move over and that the railway line is changing direction and making the gap narrow at an alarming rate. Just when we think he is going to be crushed he brakes in a cloud of dust and a squeal of brakes. It would have been difficulty to put your hand between the car and train when he eventually stopped.

A wonderfully relaxing night in a magnificent bed and another beautiful day to follow. Time to relax by the pool with a cold drink and watch an enormous tortoise and some ostriches in the hotel park before I set out for the Museo Santuarios Andinos.

A friend of mine once said, 'If you ever go to Arequipa you must see Juanita.'

In Inca times, young virgin girls were sacrificed to the gods. For the girls themselves it was a great honour, for after their death they then became immortal and lived forever with the gods. One such was Juanita. In 1992 during research work on the volcano Ampato, as part of the High Altitude Sanctuaries of Southern Andes project, the wonderfully preserved mummy of a young girl was discovered by an American archaeologist called Johan Reinhard. The grave had been disturbed by a volcanic eruption and the body lay on its side a short distance from the mountain top at a height of 21,000 feet above sea level.

The Museo Santuarios Andinos is indeed a sanctuary of peace and calm just off the main square of Arequipa, and as I pass through the gateway I leave the noise of the town behind and enter a tranquil courtyard beautifully paved, with trees and potted flowers all around. First there is a film presentation in English; it recreates the journey from the girl's village to the top of the mountain. This must have been an extremely arduous ascent, and as the girl had not been allowed to eat for some time prior to the journey she must have reached the top in a state of exhaustion. She was beautifully clothed in a long dress and shoulder wrap with a sunburst headdress. When she was arranged in her grave she was surrounded with various items that she would need in her next life.

The next stage of the presentation is a guided tour through discreetly lit rooms with glass cases. There is pottery, jewellery, cloth bags, blankets, clothes and minute figurines with incredible detail, all in remarkable condition. The colours of the textiles are as vivid as the day that they were buried. There is a definite sense of anticipation as we move from room to room and when we finally come face to face with Juanita in her glass case the sight is quite breathtaking. Automatically, people whisper.

I would describe her as beautiful, or as the dictionary would put it, 'a delight to the aesthetic senses.' She sits curled up in the same posture that she has been in for 500 years. With her bright clothes and flesh on her bones she is a fascinating sight, and it is difficult to tear yourself away.

It was definitely one of the highlights of my fifteen days in Peru.

The rest of the day passes uneventfully, and at 4 p.m. we transfer to the airport for the flight to the capital and a farewell dinner at La Rosa Nautica. This is a beautiful restaurant on the outskirts of Lima. It is built on a pier that juts out into the Pacific, and as you sit at table you can hear the waves beneath you. The food and company are excellent and there are some humorous presentations, including one for myself for having had my shoes polished more times than anyone else.

Although most of us will meet in the morning it is very much a time for saying goodbye to the new friends that I have made on this remarkable, fascinating, tiring and highly enjoyable journey. Everywhere I have met friendly and helpful people, some of whom have genuinely asked me to come again.

I have been privileged to see a remarkable country and its remarkable people, and the memory will live with me for a long time.

Colombia

It is now some time since I travelled the rail system of Peru and the start of my love affair with South America, and here I am back again, this time starting in Colombia and then moving on to Ecuador.

I suppose some would say that, in railway terms, starting with Peru would be like drinking champagne and then following it up with mineral water; but hopefully you will be able to judge for yourself by the time you have finished reading this account.

I am flying to Bogota via Paris and, as usual, it is an early start, this time at 6.30 a.m. As I kill time by wandering round the departure area I pass the only pub and it is absolutely full with five deep around the bar. There is much shouting, laughing and drinking and it is difficult to hear yourself think and I am outside. It is more like a club on Saturday night than a bar in an airport at 5.30 a.m.! Still, they all seem to be having a good time.

The plane (an Airbus A320) is on time and only half full when it leaves, and after an uneventful seventy-five minutes we touch down at a grey and wet Charles de Gaulle airport. This is my first time at this airport and I am immediately struck by the sheer scale of the place. It must be hundreds of acres in size and it resembles a gigantic building site, with half-finished buildings and cranes wherever you look. For some idea of size, it takes our plane fifteen minutes to taxi to where we disembark and then an airport bus which takes another five minutes to terminal F44, which thankfully is the same terminal that we leave from.

There are hundreds of us crowded into a security screening area that is just grey concrete and is about the most depressing place that I have ever been in. The staff are very thorough, and the man in front of me not only has to take off his hat and coat, but his belt and shoes as well.

Inside, the change is dramatic and the departure area is all steel with acres of glass. I went through three passport/security checks to get this far; maybe that is comforting, but it did create chaos. It is very clean and modern and it is easy to find your way around, unlike the walk from the bus to the security area.

On board the plane (an Airbus A340) my travelling companion is fast asleep, but as we take off he wakes up and crosses himself!

It's a ten-hour flight for the 5,375 miles from Paris to Bogota and I try to pass the time reading and tackling Sudoku puzzles. I must have dozed off for I suddenly wake up feeling as though I have been on the plane for days, but it is in fact only four hours since we took off. There is a general air of lethargy with people either asleep or watching TV.

My travelling companion has woken up and I get into conversation with him. His English is almost non-existent and we have to rely on my limited Spanish; still, it's good discipline for me to practise. He is going home after visiting relatives in France and can't wait to get back; he says that he misses the clean fresh air, the hot sun and the cleansing rain.

We are now approaching Bogota, and as we drop into the clouds the journey becomes quite scary as twice we drop like a stone and then accelerate. Suddenly we are in sunshine and I see the capital of Colombia for the first time. The city is in a great green valley and is surrounded by mountains. I can see acres of glass and my companion proudly tells me that they export flowers to Holland and all over Europe.

The landing is like a feather floating down.

Luckily, I get my suitcase quickly and am fairly near the front of the huge queues for immigration. The official is friendly but stares at me and my passport photo very intently and I start to feel guilty. I start thinking that perhaps I should have had a new passport but tell myself not to be ridiculous as it is only two years old. Suddenly, with a flourish, she stamps the passport and I am outside in the middle of a group of Colombians who are all greeting each other very passionately.

I am staying at the Tequendama/Intercontinental Hotel in Bogota and it is only about fifteen minutes from the airport. It is very grand-looking at the front and just as impressive inside, with lots of marble and nice furniture. It seems to have an army of staff.

The hotel has five stars and so, obviously, does the security, for at the front door are two very serious-looking young men in army uniform, complete with machine guns. It's difficult to know whether to feel comforted or intimidated, but I settle for comforted, as they are very willing for me to have a photograph taken with them.

I have a traditional meal in the hotel with a starter of avocado, rice and tomato followed by a main course, *ajiaco*, which is a type of stew with chicken, potatoes, onion, corn, cream, capers and

Two new friends in Bogota!

chilli sauce. The whole meal is very nice and very filling and I am happy to tumble into bed at 8.30 p.m.!

The early bed means that I am up early and I am writing these notes at four o'clock. The view from my bedroom window is of towering buildings, including a bank and a financial institution, but I remember that this is the commercial part of the city. I can already hear the sound of traffic, and although I can't see any greenery I can hear the sound of birds.

I am grateful to see that breakfast is served from 6 a.m. but can't believe that I am thinking of food so soon after that very filling meal. I had no way of knowing then that last night's meal was to be the first of a long succession of delicious local dishes that I would sample throughout Colombia and Ecuador.

After breakfast (*calvataros* - beef, kidney beans, egg and rice) it is a short bus trip to Estación de la Sabana to meet our host and guide while we are in Colombia – Eduardo. The long grey stone frontage of the station is very impressive with its many tall and arched windows.

The inside is a bit disappointing, for although there is a beautiful marble floor with several very Grecian columns and an ornate staircase, the whole scene has an air of dirt and neglect. My initial impression of Estación de la Sabana was of a run-down Greek temple.

The station café is doing a roaring trade and all round its walls are pictures of the railway history of Bogota, together with photos of derelict steam locomotives that have since been restored to full working order.

Our locomotive, which is simmering in the station, is No. 76, a 4–8–0 Baldwin. There is a beautiful polished brass plate on the front with the number on and also a big shiny brass bell on the top of the boiler. The locomotive has been freshly cleaned and painted, and with a fluttering flag at each side of the smoke box door and very large headlamps the overall picture is very pleasing.

Eduardo now takes us on a tour of the loco shed and work-shop. The building itself has definitely seen better days with gaping

Customers in the cafe

holes and flapping corrugated sheets on the roof. The derelict locomotives and coaches inside look, to me, to be well past any hope of restoration, but Eduardo croons over them as though they were his children and speaks of the time when they will run again.

I now get an insight into Eduardo's skill, knowledge and commitment. He is a partner in a company that runs the *Tren Turistico* and they regularly run steam-hauled trips around the Bogota Savanna at $24 a head for adults. His commitment and dedication to restoring derelict steam locomotives is phenomenal, and he has now fully restored two Baldwins, both of which, in the process, he has converted back from oil-burning to coal-fired! When I ask him why, he says that it is not only because he has a passion for steam locomotives, but also because Colombia has a plentiful supply of coal, and it is far cheaper than diesel. He goes on to say that he learned a lot of his skills in England and spent several years there working on locomotives, although they were

Eduardo at home in his workshop

nearly always diesel. Most of his time in England was in Sheffield and Manchester, but he has also been to other rail centres such as Crewe.

He lovingly shows me the antiquated equipment that he uses in restoration and it is remarkable just how much of what is needed, either new or repaired, is done 'in-house'. When I look at the pristine No. 76 outside it is very difficult to imagine that it once looked like the decrepit locomotive that is in front of me at the moment.

Eduardo's attitude towards his work is an equal mixture of passion and professionalism, and at sixty-nine his energy seems undiminished; he speaks with pride of his son, Andreas, who has the same enthusiasm and commitment as himself.

It's time for photographs of the train starting from the station, and as she slowly pulls out, belching great clouds of black smoke, the driver is continually operating both the whistle and the bell. The noise must be heard for miles around.

The old and the new

Leaving Bogota

The smell of the smoke is very evocative and takes me back many years, both to my childhood and the time when I worked on the railways.

There are several of us in the observation car at the back of the train, and it appears to be turning into a drinking den. I am being persuaded by our host to drink Nectar (*aguardiente*). It is a Colombian liquor and very strong. My notes remind me that I had reached a point (five glasses) where I was starting to laugh too much, and I turned to coffee instead.

Eduardo tells me that the track in Colombia is owned by one company and his company have to pay to run trains on it. He talks of the condition of the track, which is causing us to travel quite slowly, about ten to fifteen miles per hour. He goes on to say that he had special dispensation to run this train out of Estación de la Sabana today, as the station is currently closed to the travelling public because of the poor condition of the track for the first few miles out of the station.

San Antonio graveyard

We have been travelling for about seven or eight miles and are still in Bogota and the track is now an island sandwiched between a dual carriageway. We are now passing San Antonio station (closed) and a little further on there is an enormous graveyard; it covers acres and acres and there are literally hundreds of people about. There are no gravestones, only little plaques set in the grass with people sitting around them. The grass is beautifully mown and there are yellow roses, red oleander and many other coloured shrubs. The sun is shining and the scene is very picturesque and it is difficult to see it as a place of sadness.

We have now made a stop at Usaquen Station. This is partly to let a freight train through, but it also gives us the opportunity of buying some souvenirs from the station shop. All the souvenirs are actually about Tren Turistico de la Sabana, as this station is where Eduardo's office is situated!

My souvenir is a baseball-type cap with 'Turistren Bogota-Colombia' on the front, actually a gift from Eduardo.

Usaquen Station

I pick up one of Eduardo's leaflets, and in one it says:

Disfruta de un bello recorrido – Ayuda a preserver la tradición.

My probably poor translation is:

Enjoy a beautiful trip, help preserve a tradition.

My sentiments exactly!

Usaquen Station is a very pretty two-storey building with a single storey at the side for the office and café. Its white painted walls with green edging and red roof tiles remind me very much of an Alpine house from a different part of the world, and I look forward to the photograph.

Leaving Usaquen

The next stop is Cajica. This attractive town has a very pretty central plaza with palm trees, benches and flowering shrubs.

The whole scene is quite vibrant, with people relaxing and enjoying the warm sunshine, others shopping, some just strolling

Welcome to Cajica

about, and there is also a large crowd at the central church where a funeral service is taking place. On a nearby bench a young couple are sitting entwined, with eyes only for each other.

There is a festival here today, and the local population will soon

Arriving at Cajica

be swelled by a few hundred more as there is a train expected shortly which will bring people in from the Bogota area.

The smoke and shrieking whistle of the train is seen and heard long before its arrival, and when it does arrive it is a wonderful sight. Another immaculate steam locomotive is pulling fourteen coaches which are painted in all the colours of the rainbow, and each coach has a huge painted logo advertising products such as KitKat and Nestlé.

We have lunch at the Jica Restaurant in the central plaza, and enjoy yet another nice local dish with the main part being a superb steak. There is live traditional music throughout the meal and afterwards I am presented with a locust made out of leaves and sticks. It is beautifully made and now sits on my mantelpiece at home.

As I stroll about the town after lunch I meet nothing but friendliness from the local people, and the stares that I see are of curiosity not hostility.

The people from the train have now been in town about three hours and will shortly return to La Caro. Eduardo says that it will be a wonderful Colombian experience for us to travel on this train with them and share not only their excitement but also to enjoy the several groups of musicians that will also be on the train and

Students in Cajica

94

The train crew at Cajica

will move back and forth along the coaches, giving a few minutes' performance in each.

In the event, the experience of that journey was one not to be missed. Each group has different types of musicians and the

Leaving Cajica

Music while you travel

instruments are many and varied – some wind, some guitars, some pan pipes and most of them with vocals as well. They all play with great volume and enthusiasm, and it is a pleasure to be part of it. I have a tape recording of it that I am listening to as I write these notes.

At La Caro, our fellow passengers leave for their return to Bogota, which will be in several very brightly-coloured, open-sided buses that are all lined up alongside the railway. The buses are all American and of a 1940s vintage.

All change at La Caro

96

By the buses there is a band playing; the musicians are all wearing what looks to be full evening costume. The whole scene is one of colour, excitement, activity and enjoyment, and I would like to sum up the atmosphere – in a very complimentary way – as typically South American.

Party time at Le Caro

We have now transferred by bus to a town called Briceno. It is raining quite heavily and there is not much enthusiasm to explore. I can see what turns out to be a children's adventure playground. There is a white Taj Mahal-type building with many towers and minarets, and in front of it there is a huge statue about 40 foot high with a spiked headdress; the detail of the statue is both good and proportionate, and he is obviously male!

We have now transferred by train from Briceno back to La Caro, and because of time limitations are returning to Bogota by coach rather than train. It is raining, dark and cold all the way back to Bogota, and there is not much to see, apart from one couple at the roadside under what appears to be a home-made gazebo; they have a roaring fire, over which are hung several large pieces of meat, presumably for sale. The only other remarkable thing about this journey is the time that it takes from the outskirts of Bogota to our hotel, about three-quarters of an hour. Bogota (population 8 million) seems to stretch for miles and miles and as you get into the suburbs there are six or seven lanes of traffic all taking you to the centre. In addition, there are dedicated bus lanes carrying the Trans Milenio both into and out of the city, and those buses appear to race up and down all the time. I speculate idly how you would cross these roads on foot.

I had a restless night last night and didn't sleep very well. I was awake at 1.40 a.m., 2.40 a.m. and finally 4.40 a.m., when I gave in and got up. I don't understand why I am not sleeping well, as Bogota is only 8,500 feet above sea level and I coped with greater altitudes than this when I was in Peru.

I am on the eleventh floor, and looking down at 5.45 a.m. I can see, a long way down, about fifteen soldiers who are obviously getting ready for the day's duties. They are all wearing helmets with 'MP' on and are also carrying machine guns; I am already thinking of this as the norm and think no more about it.

Early morning Bogota

Sometime in the night somebody pushed a bill under my door for 10,000 pesos for the mini bar. I haven't used it and I see from my notes that my response at the time was 'bloody cheek'! This comment was probably because of lack of sleep.

Down for breakfast at 6.00 a.m., I have the *calvataros* again, together with fresh pineapple, pineapple juice and yoghurt. It seems like the two ends of the healthy eating syndrome.

Good Morning Bogota!

After breakfast we leave by coach and arrive at La Caro at 9.30 a.m. on a beautiful sunny morning in time for our train to Zipaquira. The countryside between La Caro and Cajica is very lush and green and there are also a lot of eucalyptus trees. We have just crossed a little bridge, and on the right I can see lots of horses. One of them gets very excited at our noisy approach and races round and round the field in quite a frantic manner; the driver sounding the whistle doesn't help, either. The fields around Cajica are a mass of daisies, buttercups and clover, and with the tree-covered hills as a backdrop the whole scene evokes thoughts of my childhood.

Harvesting Eucalyptus trees

Some miles later and we have stopped for a line-side photograph; the train has just emerged from a tree-lined avenue into an area of rolling fields stretching away to the mountains behind. It is a very panoramic and attractive view.

The panoramic view

It's a testament to Eduardo

A geological vision

Beautiful flowers

We are on the edge of a small town, and just ahead of us is a metallurgical factory with mountains of pipes, iron filings and other scrap metal. Behind a high security fence two guards, one armed with a shotgun and the other with a handgun, are making a fuss of a large Rottweiler. The dog is a big softy with them, but I bet he wouldn't be if I was in there!

We are now running alongside the main road and it is like a scene from an American 'road' film with all the huge Dodge and Ford transporters alongside us. I have just seen a very ancient Buick, and although he passed us, it was only just!

We are now about three miles from Zipaquira, and Eduardo says that there is a good gradient just ahead, and I will not only

Cerrada

get a good photograph of the train working hard, but I will also be able to get a good sound recording. I am listening to that sound as I write these notes and it is a very happy memory, not just of Colombia but also of times in my childhood when I used

Zipaquira

Zipaquira from the Salt Mine

to listen to Castle Locomotives tackling Gresford Bank in North Wales.

Seventy kilometres from Bogota is Zipaquira, and in the hills behind the town is their famous salt cathedral which we are going to visit. There is a long steep winding road from the town that ends at the gateway of a working salt mine at one side and the entrance and car park to the salt cathedral on the other. Zipaquira and miles of surrounding countryside are laid out far below us.

At this moment all I know about the salt cathedral is that it is deep underground, carved from solid salt, and was opened to the public in 1995. There is no longer any extraction of salt from this part of the mine and it is now entirely a religious tourist attraction. There is wide sloping walkway leading into a long dark tunnel, and as we go deeper the head-room varies between about eight feet and thirty feet. The whole complex is a former salt mine, and the tour follows a series of worked-out chambers carved from the salt. Each of these galleries has a cross at the entrance and depicts a stage in Christ's walk to his crucifixion.

Each gallery is very high and brightly lit at the front, but the back is always shrouded in darkness; in answer to a question I learn that each gallery is about 400 feet long.

We have just entered a big round open gallery. This is where the choir stands, and a long way below us is the actual cathedral with rows of pews leading to the altar and a huge cross about fifty feet high. The cross is carved from the salt in such a way that it seems, from our viewpoint, as though it is hollowed out from the salt rather than the other way round. It is a very impressive optical illusion.

The journey from the entrance to this point is 700 metres.

I follow a steep flight of steps down for what seems a very long way and suddenly I am in the cathedral. Close by there is a side chapel to the Virgin of the Salt. It is a working cathedral, and immensely impressive by its sheer scale and method of construction. There are four huge pillars, also carved from salt, and these reach to the ceiling. I am standing near the altar which is carved from a thirty-ton block of salt, and nearby is the area for baptism; all baptisms are done with salt water.

Monument to the Salt Miners

The ceiling of the cathedral at this point must be about seventy or eighty feet above us and the acoustics are absolutely wonderful.

The drive back down to the town is very attractive as there are nice gardens, and nice houses and restaurants; it is quite a contrast with the rest of the town.

We are due to fly to Guayaquil in Ecuador tonight, and as a time-filler we have a short tour of old Bogota; it is a great pity that by the time that we get there it too dark for photographs and also to fully appreciate what is obviously a very attractive place, with balconied buildings, nice museums, really old and interesting houses and a large and impressive central plaza.

It is now time to say goodbye, after our all too short visit to Colombia, and transfer to the airport for our 10.30 p.m. flight to Guayaquil in Ecuador.

Ecuador

Guayaquil was named after a Huancavelica chief, Guayas, and his princess wife, Quil. An ancient legend says that he killed his wife and then drowned himself in the river that bears his name; he did this in preference to surrendering to the Spaniards.

The plane is a McDonnell Douglas 83, and we take off at 10.45 p.m. and are due to land at Guayaquil at midnight.

My journey is very noisy as the engine is mounted right outside the window where I am sitting, so that not only are my ears assaulted but there is also no view from the window.

The transfer to the Grand Hotel takes about an hour and I am thankful to eventually tumble into bed at about 1.30 a.m.

I am woken this morning at just after six o'clock by the shrill cheeping of a bird outside. It's a very insistent sound and typical of the jungle, even though the hotel is in the heart of the city.

The hotel was built in 1975 and is close to most of the important plazas, churches, monuments, museums and public spaces of this great port city.

From my window I can see an enclosed area made up of three sides of the hotel and the fourth side is the end wall of the Cathedral. This wall and the surrounding area are covered with lush green vegetation which is designed to emulate the jungle; somewhere in the greenery my avian early morning call is perched.

There is a sun terrace and in one corner there is a cascade tumbling down to an inviting pool. The whole scene is one of beauty and tranquillity.

Breakfast and a 9 a.m. start. Although the Ecuador railway is

Guayaquil Cathedral

known as 'The Guayaquil and Quito Railway', it doesn't actually start from Guayaquil but starts from a place called Duran across the Guayas River.

Our coach takes us past the Malecon, where I walked yesterday, and a little further on by the airport we turn left on the first of two bridges. The first bridge spans the River Daule, and the road then continues across what is an island called La Puntilla, and then across another bridge that this time spans the River Babahoyo. The crossing is immensely busy and there are three solid lanes of traffic going each way; there is also construction under way to widen the bridge still further.

As the two rivers pass La Puntilla they merge to form the River Guayas.

We are now in Duran.

The station at Duran has been shut for some time and rail access to it has now been permanently closed by tarmac on the roads and some buildings on the rail route out of the station. The station itself is in a very poor state of repair and part of the former

Street market at Duran

station area is now what seems to be a repair centre for amusement rides for small children.

Any trains now leaving Duran do so from the loco shed and workshop about half a mile away from the station, and our train, a red Baldwin 2–6–0 with the number '11' on the front, is gently simmering outside the shed. The loco yard is a desolate sight, with overgrown tracks and rusting wagons and tankers. There is also a long line of rusting ferry boats, economic victims of the bridge that was built to span the two rivers between Guayaquil and Duran.

There are also some very tired-looking banana palms growing against the wall of the workshop.

On the side of the locomotive there is a plaque that says that it was reconstructed in March 1955. She is oil-fired, which surprises me as I had expected a coal-fired locomotive, but the steam and smoke are just as realistic, with only the smell of burning oil to give the game away.

Behind the locomotive is a large tanker carrying its water supply,

109

Can I come too!

as any water columns on the line have long since gone. The passenger accommodation is rudimentary and is made up of two open wagons with bench seating down each side and a tin roof. There are no windows or doors and it is just a question of grab a rail and climb aboard.

Belching an enormous cloud of black smoke, the locomotive emerges from the yard gates directly on to a main road. There is no traffic control and it is just a question of all traffic having to give way to the shriek of the train's whistle.

We have crossed the road and are now running down the middle of the town high street; we are creating quite a stir and within minutes the second wagon is full to overflowing with passengers of all ages having a free ride. The roofs of both wagons are also covered with people. There is no question of stopping; is just a matter of climb aboard as and when you can.

We have barely travelled a mile when we get our first derailment; it is the water tanker, which is obviously the heaviest vehicle of the train. Instantly, there is a crowd of onlookers, together with the more enterprising element who turn up selling ice cream, cool

Leaving Duran

drinks and melon pieces. The track is in terrible condition and it seems amazing to me that we have managed to travel even a mile on it.

One of the train crew produces a block of metal shaped like a wedge of cheese and the job of re-railing begins. There is a lot of activity, and talking and every so often the locomotive belches black smoke and, with spinning wheels, tries to drag the tanker back on to the track. After about three-quarters of an hour they are finally successful and a tape measure is then produced to

That's about right

Spectators

111

measure the rail gauge, which has been distorted with all the pushing and pulling.

The next bit, as the train crew attempt to fix the rails, probably sums up the state of the G & Q. Most of the sleepers are either rotten or missing, and there are very few track-fixing pins and the crew resort to hunting round for pieces of wood to use as track pins. These are either branches pulled from a tree or pieces of wood lying by the track side, and in either case they are totally inadequate! With no effort it is possible to push the track out of gauge with a very small pressure of your foot.

Nevertheless, I am full of admiration for the train crew, who have performed the feat of re-railing with nothing more than a piece of metal cheese and a few small blocks of wood, plus a lot of shouting and arm-waving.

Today we are only travelling the section from Duran to Yaguachi (twenty-one kilometres), as the line is severed between Yaguachi and Bucay. At the time of writing this travelogue there are several sections of the G & Q closed to all traffic, and I will list the details of these at the end.

For now, the reason for the section being closed between Yaguachi and Bucay is that, in 1999, the then Mayor of Milagro decided that he did not want dirty, smoky trains travelling up and down the middle of his High Street, and he therefore pulled up all the tracks! They haven't yet been replaced, although he is no longer mayor of that town. It could only happen in South America!

The area between Duran and Bucay is flat lowland, and as we clear the outskirts of Duran there are bamboo and rush work houses close to the line. The bamboo comes from trees that are about nine inches across, and when they are cut down they are then sliced into strips which are then bound together to form the walls of the houses.

This line of houses goes on for mile after mile and they all appear to be in a dilapidated condition. However, the people in them are dressed smartly, look happy and cheerful, and have turned

One more push

out in their hundreds to wave at the train which is rattling along at about ten miles an hour.

There are literally hundreds of children, and I don't think that I have ever seen so many at any one time. The passing of the train is obviously a major event for all of them, and many of the

Tables

children climb on and off the train as it travels along – a true spectator sport!

We have reached a wide and modern tarmac main road and it is decided to take the opportunity for a run-by photograph on the crossing.

Again, it could only be in South America, as the train is left halfway across the road while the taking of the photograph is discussed. Some traffic goes around the train while others just wait until, without warning, the train starts to back up across the road for its run past. The wonderful thing about the whole episode is that nobody is impatient, angry or anxious.

We are now entering an area of much cultivation and there are rice fields everywhere, with all the small villages and individual houses built on stilts. It all looks fairly dry but in the rainy season, soon to arrive, this will all be water as far as the eye can see. The houses are built on stilts – not just to be above the water in the rainy season but also to be above the snakes in the dry season!

We are just passing a green rice paddy and in the middle of it

High and dry

I can see a large number of white egrets. They are quite motionless and unmoved by our noisy passing. We have now reached Yaguachi, and on the edge of town a black river flows sluggishly under the girders of the railway bridge. It looks an absolute haven for mosquitoes.

The bridge at Yaguachi

The noise and smoke of our train has gone before us, and as we enter the town it looks as though the entire population has turned out to meet us. Yaguachi is quite a substantial town but looks very poor.

As the train runs down the middle of the high street we are

Turning the train at Yaguachi

Yaguachi main street

pursued by hordes of people and it is an absolute party for the locals: ride on the train, chase the train, laugh at the train…

At the far end of town the train pulls up and it is time for a boxed lunch. The stop gives the local children the chance to climb all over the train and there are literally dozens of them. The locomotive and its wagons are like a new centrepiece in a children's play park, and they are on it, under it, on top of it, round it, in it, everywhere.

With much shrieking of the whistle, the train now manages to clear a path for the return journey to Duran, but first there will be a run-past photo opportunity.

The whole town now seems to be waiting, with people staring down from the balconies of their precarious-looking houses and the bicycle taxis motionless.

Even the children are now still. It is as though some momentous event is about to happen; perhaps it is, and they are all waiting to say goodbye to this noisy, smoke belching monster that briefly invaded their town. As I stand idly waiting, a cyclist flashes past at an amazing speed. His head is down and there is a look of

116

Relaxation and arrival at Casiguama

fierce concentration on his face. He is holding the handlebars with one hand and in the other he is holding a crutch. He has only got one leg but is putting tremendous energy into his ride and the vacant pedal is whirling round.

It's about midday, and we have made a brief stop at an isolated station called Casiguama. On a siding there is a four-wheeled inspection trolley with the handlebar that you pump up and down to make it go, and the hordes of children that we are still carrying soon have it going along the rails.

The only building that I can see in the area is the station house, and outside there is an old man relaxing in a hammock. He seems totally unmoved by our arrival.

A girl of about fifteen appears out of the house and starts to climb over the front of the locomotive. She is quite skimpily dressed and delights in posing for people who want to take photographs; she is quite attractive and maybe it will be her career one day.

We are about halfway now and have reached the main road where we had our earlier photo stop; there is a choice here of staying on the train to Duran or returning by a coach that is following us. I opt for the coach, partly because I feel that I have had enough of being shaken and rattled all day, but mainly because if I go back on the coach it will be so much quicker that I will have an additional two or three hours in which to explore Guayaquil.

After a tiring day I now have an opportunity to explore a little

117

of this very interesting city. Immediately behind the hotel is the magnificent neo-Gothic cathedral with its twin spires, and just across the road is Iguana Park; this small park is very well named as I can see at least ten to a dozen of these interesting creatures, with the longest one being about four or five feet.

Iguana Park at Guayaquil

The iguanas are fed by the local authority and show no inclination to wander from their very attractive surroundings. They coexist very happily with the people sitting on benches talking, or those just strolling like me.

A few minutes' walk from here and I am at the Malecon 2000. This is a huge public works project that stretches for one and a half miles along the waterfront and covers an area of about forty-two acres. There are three sections to the Malecon, and I enter at the southern end where the old market is situated, not far from the impressive City Hall. This splendid building has a Greek-style frontage with many columns, although domes on the corners look more Moorish than Greek.

Moored at the quayside opposite City Hall is the *Guayas* teaching ship, belonging to the Ecuadorian Navy. This tall sailing ship, with its furled sails, polished masts and spars and white painted hull, is a graceful sight.

As I stand admiring this lovely craft, a frigate bird glides effortlessly by.

Also in the southern section is the Bahia Malecon shopping

The Guayas

centre. This is a very modern piece of architecture with lots of glass and a terrace of restaurants overlooking the Guayas River.

You can stroll along the broad promenade with its beautiful coloured paving, interspersed with timber walkways, or you can walk through the different gardens that run through the whole length of the Malecon.

The Malecon

These gardens have different themes both in types of trees and shrubs and also in countries of origin. I find it very difficult to realise that I am only yards away from the hustle and bustle of a busy city as I stroll through the peace and tranquillity of these green spaces.

The central area is essentially historic and I have paused to study and take a photograph of Hemiciclo de la Rotonda. This semicircular monument, with its two statues, was erected in 1937 to commemorate the meeting of Simon Bolivar and San Martin, two Latin American liberators.

The northern section of the Malecon has space for sports, aerobics, skating and entertainment, together with science and art. There is a very attractive water fountain.

There is also a garden here that holds diverse plant species of the Ecuadorian coast, and I think, as I always do in places like this. Why can't I grow some of these at home!

Although I already knew that it was there, I suddenly come across an old first-class railway coach sitting on an isolated piece of track. From the outside it looks like it always probably did, and when I peep inside (it's locked) the only change there is that all the original seating has been taken out and replaced with loose tables and chairs, with a computer on each table. It is an information centre.

I have been aiming for the Las Peñas neighbourhood at the extreme northern end, but time is against me and I now turn back. Las Peñas is the first residential area of Guayaquil and is reached by climbing almost 500 steps up Santa Ana Hill. Although this area has existed since colonial times, Las Peñas was completely destroyed by fire in 1896 and rebuilt in a neoclassical style.

We have an early start tomorrow and I will not see Guayaquil again, which is a pity because there is so much to see and do in this absorbing city.

Today we are travelling from Guayaquil to Bucay by coach, a distance of about eighty-five kilometres.

On the way out of the city and we are now passing a cemetery. It covers an enormous area and from what I can see from the coach it looks like a miniature city with huge mausoleums and elaborate tombs; they are all linked with roadways but without traffic, for the population of this place have long ago reached their destination. As we leave the city area, the road follows the railway and the landscape gradually changes to huge sugar cane plantations. There must be thousands of acres because in some places they stretch as far as the eye can see, and in some parts the road is an island between two banks of canes ten foot high waving in the breeze. All this vast lowland used to be tropical rainforest but my imagination cannot recreate that image. As if to confirm that refusal there suddenly appears a huge factory, belching smoke.

It is a sugar cane processing factory and inside the factory compound there is a long line of lorries piled high with cut cane that is waiting its turn to be devoured and then turned into sugar for those people with a sweet tooth. On the other side of the road there is another access to the factory, and in the undergrowth,

The sugar loco

covered in brambles and bushes, there is an abandoned steam locomotive. It is an old privately-owned sugar cane locomotive with '*Ingenio Valdez*' (the owners) on the side. Its number is 55298 and it was built in 1922.

We have just time to take a couple of photos before armed guards come and order us to leave.

Not for nothing is Milagro known as the sugar cane and pineapple capital of Ecuador, and as we make a brief comfort stop in the town I can see an enormous pineapple made out of stainless steel. It must be at least twenty feet high and it is decorating a roundabout at the end of the road.

The Pineapple and new friends at Milagro

The next fifty kilometres between here and Bucay is across flat tropical lowland interspersed with large cattle ranches, small towns and enormous plantations of exotic fruits and trees. All this was once tropical rainforest, and now only about 10 per cent of Ecuador's rainforest survives. The main plantations are mainly bananas and pineapples and these stretch for many miles, but there also plenty of smaller plantations with mangos, tangerines, papaya, melon and cacao trees. We have also just passed a place where there is a large plantation of teak trees on one side of the road and balsa trees on the other.

Every so often we pass a lorry laden to the gunnels with exotic fruit and there are also occasional small hangars for the crop-dusting planes.

We have now just crossed the Chan Chan River and are in Bucay. Ecuador is divided into provinces, and in crossing the river we have passed into a new province; this one is called Guayas Province. Suddenly the smooth tarmac road becomes uneven and pitted with potholes, and the houses are also now very poor-looking; this all reflects the amount of wealth in different provinces.

Bucay is a reasonably-sized town with a long main street with several shops. Although there are some people about there is a very somnolent air about the place with just the occasional bicycle taxi and a group of children leaving school.

Bucay main street

I have my boxed lunch sitting on a wall by the loco shed. It is extremely hot and I am very glad of my hat.

This trip by coach means that we have missed out the stations of Milagro, Naranjito and Barraganetal on the isolated rail section from Yaguachi to Bucay. The next part of the journey will be from here to Huigra by railcar, with an overnight stop at the Luis Antonio Hosteria in the rainforest. Tomorrow there will be another coach trip from Bucay to Alausi where we pick up a steam train for the assault on the Devil's Nose.

At the end of this account of my journey there is detailed information on the operational situation of the Guayaquil-Quito Railway.

Bucay locomotive shed is a huge barn of a place constructed from actual rails and corrugated iron sheets. The place is black, dilapidated and filthy dirty, and the steam locomotives that are sitting inside have obviously not moved for some years.

They are all Baldwins, and are No. 44, 2–8–0; No. 58, 2–8–0 and No. 46, 2–6–0, and have all been rendered useless by the fact that Bucay is almost a railway island in the country's rail system.

All the tracks outside are overgrown with weeds and there are deserted boxcars and wagons parked here and there. It is still very hot and I make for the shade between an old boxcar and the wall at the edge of the yard. Somebody is there before me but is relieving himself against the boxcar and I make a retreat. On the other side I look for somewhere else, but then become aware that there is someone asleep under the boxcar, despite what is happening to him on the other side. The whole thing has a somewhat surreal air.

Forty winks

124

The railcar is a bus welded onto a set of rail bogies. It is now standing in the closed and deserted station, which is adjacent to the rail yard. I have decided to travel this next section on the roof, for on Ecuadorian railways anything goes!

Our departure from Bucay is a comparatively quiet affair and I try to make myself comfortable on the roof … not easy! The line climbs all the way out of the town and soon we are in an area of fairly lush vegetation with a river following us in a deep valley on first one side and then the other. We cross the river four times on this thirty-kilometre section of the trip. On both sides of us are towering mountains.

The areas of lush vegetation are interspersed with burnt patches where the Indians have burnt off the surface vegetation in order that grass can then grow to feed their animals.

This practice, in conjunction with deforestation, has had a dramatic effect on the stability of many of the mountainsides, and it is a major contributor to the frequent landslides.

The driver of the railcar tells me a story about a time a few months ago when he came up this line and found that a fire that the Indians had started had also ignited the railway sleepers and they were burning merrily, they had to go back and when they returned the following day they were still burning and so they returned again for water to put them out.

It is difficult to see how this line survives. The sleepers are more like logs and the rails are certainly not straight, they twist and bend and are rusty-looking. It looks more like an abandoned mine track back home that has not been run on for thirty years and has just been left.

It is lovely to see bananas, oranges and mangos growing wild.

Huigra is a small dusty town wedged in a narrow valley between the mountains, and the railway runs through the middle of it. There is no rush of people to see the train, and although the station itself looks fairly neat and tidy, it is not clear whether it is actually open for business, although two men that I later get into conversation with tell me that two railcars a week come from Bucay.

New friends in Huigra

The same two men also tell me that the population of this town is only 800, and that they have concern that the drain of young people to the larger towns is having a bad effect on Huigra and its prosperity. They are both about thirty years old and are very happy in their town, and also tell me that they have no police there because there is no crime.

Students in Huigra

126

A little way from the station is a large colonial-type building that at first glance seems deserted but is in fact a technical college.

I am suddenly joined by a giggling group of girls of about sixteen, all immaculately dressed in uniform. They are returning to college for the last session of the day, and are curious to know who I am. They are very interested that I am an English tourist.

They are very pleased to have their photograph taken, and as I look through the lens I am reminded that in all the places that I have seen, no matter how poor the living conditions, the children are always immaculately turned out in uniform for school.

We are now on the way back, and after a few kilometres have made a short stop. It turns out that the driver wants to show us some pieces of metal at the line side. He takes pleasure in telling us that this is where a railcar took a bend too fast and came off; he was a bit vague about injuries. A littler further on and we stop again to view more remains, and have the same story again. It was the same in Peru, where they always seemed to be anxious to point out where crashes or derailments had occurred.

We will be stopping for the night at the Luis Antonio Hosteria, which is about halfway between Huigra and Bucay. It is only accessible by rail, and although the owner has a four-by-four car,

The way in and out

Luis Antonio Hosteria

he has to drive on the rails for some distance to and from the Hosteria; this includes a river bridge where he has laid planking between the rails in order that he can drive across.

The position of the Hosteria is idyllic and the whisper of nearby water is very pleasing.

There is no vehicle access here, only rail, and the surroundings are of tropical rainforest with all the attendant creature sounds. The building itself is mostly timber and blends well with its surroundings.

Hidden on a lower level is a swimming pool and Turkish bath, and lower still, a pond stocked with exotic fish set in a garden where a path winds between colourful shrubs and trees.

The Luis Antonio Hosteria is also a centre for many physical activities. There is a spectacular waterfall, where the braver elements can leap from the top into the cool green waters below – only for the brave, I think.

Alas, my bedroom is very poor. With the Hosteria's location I had expected the facilities to be a bit basic, but not this bad. The mattress is quite thin and very hard and offers no comfort at all.

The shower is an electrician's nightmare with bare wires leading to the motor on the shower head.

I am too hot and sticky to be choosy but I am not happy about using it. In the morning, there is no hot water for a shave, or a kettle to boil any.

I am glad to leave in the morning; this is a pity because it is truly a beautiful location.

The journey to Bucay is soon over and we are now transferring to a coach for our trip to Alausi. As we have now entered the foothills of the Andes, it seems a good moment to comment on the lowlands that we have just left.

All the thousands of square miles that form the lowlands of Ecuador have been deforested for agriculture. This policy has resulted in a change in the ecosystem, as the lowlands have now changed from a humid and tropical area to one that is very dry. Although it seems a shame to have destroyed all that rainforest, this comment is not intended as a criticism, as the country needed to improve its economy and saw the lowlands as a valuable resource to that end.

Alausi is a very pleasant mountain town (7,655 feet above sea level) with a wide main street and many shops, together with a purpose-built indoor market. The hotel is small but comfortable, and dinner tonight is alfresco fronting the main street. This is very pleasant, and it is interesting to people-watch. Two young men cruise up and down the street in a Chevrolet pickup followed by two more young men cruising in a black Chevrolet car. Across the street there is a band playing and there is much singing; it must be possible to hear them all over the town. There is a general air of relaxation and enjoyment.

Up at 6.30 a.m. to a beautiful sunny morning, and already there are plenty of people about. The girl at the hotel desk is called Lucia, and she is very keen to practise English and bombards me with, 'Who are you? Where you go? Where you from?'

Lucia is proud of her town and is happy to give me directions about where and what to see. It's my impression that although she does not want to leave Alausi she craves information about people and places beyond Ecuador. It is a great experience for two people from different continents to meet and for each to seek knowledge about the other.

A lesson there somewhere in this difficult world.

Near the hotel there is a place (they have signs outside them saying 'Cabins') where you can make telephone calls both locally and nationally, basically it is a room with three or four telephone booths and a small office with a computer. You make your call, and the time and cost is monitored by a person at the computer and you pay him when you have finished. The system is very easy and ludicrously cheap, and my call to the UK of about six minutes costs me less than £1.

Today our steam train is taking us on the short eleven-kilometre trip to Sibambe and back, via the Devil's Nose. The distance between Sibambe and Alausi may be short, but on that return trip we will have to climb nearly 1,700 feet.

There are many sharp curves on this section until suddenly the Devil's Nose (*El Nariz del Diablo*) comes into view. When the engineers built this line they were faced with the decision of

Leaving Alausi

Alausi to Sibambe

whether to go over or around this immense obstacle. As a train ride it is an exhilarating experience, but for the efficient transfer of freight or passengers, it is sadly inadequate, and I think that its survival, or not, can only be through tourism.

To overcome this huge natural barrier, the engineers decided to traverse the almost perpendicular side of the mountain by the construction of two spectacular zigzags, and as we come round the base of the mountain I can see the river in the valley floor and beyond that the former station of Sibambe.

When we reach the extent of the first zigzag, the points are changed, and the train is now reversing down to the next one where the process is repeated and we are now running loco first into Sibambe.

Sibambe is a former junction and the station buildings are an island between two tracks; the one to the right went on to Bucay and Guayaquil and the one to the left formerly went to Cuenca; that line is unfortunately no longer operational because of landslips.

On the devil's nose

Sibambe was never much more than a station and was mainly used as a meeting place for farmers on their way to the city markets. The two ornate pillars that used to support the roof of the booking hall are still there but the roof is long gone, as it has

Sibambe station

from the adjoining two-storey administrative and office building and both buildings are now just empty shells.

I have my lunch beside the river while the locomotive also has its refreshment via a long pipe down to the water. It is incredibly peaceful here and the only sound is from the locomotive gently hissing in the background. On either side of me the mountains tower above this very narrow valley, which has room for the river and the railway and nothing else.

The return journey up the Devil's Nose is somewhat slower but just as enjoyable, and I sit back and relax to enjoy the short but steep climb back to Alausi.

This morning our train will take us from the beautiful setting of Alausi to Guamote, on the next leg of this tour of Ecuador by rail, but first I have a couple of hours to look around the town.

For the first time I manage to get a shoeshine, and as the man transforms my grimy footwear I talk with his companion, who is a local girl of about seventeen. She is attending college on a three-year tourism course. Her name is Natalie and she is very glad of the opportunity to practise her small amount of English.

There are not many customers in the local market but plenty of stalls, mostly selling fruit and vegetables. I fancy some bananas, and the opportunity to again talk with local people, but the stall that I choose was a mistake for a conversational exchange. It was, however, both entertaining and highly enjoyable. The lady in charge is dressed in the colourful clothes and the ubiquitous trilby, and it turns out that not only does she not speak English but her Spanish is very limited and she speaks only in her natural tongue of Quechua. The buying of bananas is easy but conversation soon becomes a matter of great hilarity, as my limited Spanish and sign gestures and her Quechua language are proving very entertaining for the other stallholders around us.

Even without language, it soon becomes obvious to me that the other stallholders are teasing this one about her having made a

My Quechua friend

conquest with me, for she is showing signs of being flustered. The whole episode has only lasted a few minutes but it strikes me that everybody has had an extremely enjoyable experience in that short time.

Plaza Bolivar, Alausi

I have found my way to Plaza Bolivar and it is a very pleasant spot. A sign says that it was constructed in 2004, and with the attractive paving and colourful flower borders it is tempting to just sit and relax; I have the plaza to myself, and on this beautiful warm and cloudless day, with the town surrounded by mountains, I do just that.

Although the plaza is a new affair, there is a timeless feeling to it all as I sit there.

Out of a doorway across the street, a man suddenly emerges with a cockerel in his arms and I watch him with some curiosity. With a piece of string about five feet long, he tethers it to a bolt set into the wall, puts a handful of corn down and leaves. As I am wondering why he couldn't find some more congenial surroundings for the cockerel, he returns with another one and tethers this cockerel about ten feet further along. He repeats this three more times, and there are now five cockerels busily pecking away in the sunshine. This is obviously a regular occurrence as the bolts in the wall have clearly been there for some time.

It's time to see what is happening at the station. On the way I buy some freshly-made bread rolls; they are warm and absolutely delicious.

The scene at the station is one of tremendous activity. At one end of the station in a siding there is a garishly painted brand new railcar; our steam train is standing at the platform with our shadow railcar in another siding, and at the other end of the station there is a diesel locomotive waiting to come through. It is pulling several boxcars, all of which have their roofs crowded with people.

The station square is full of onlookers and the platform is crowded with people trying to sell things, including coffee, sweets, flags, train driver's hats, maps, etc. There is also a stall selling handcrafted items made out of the kernel of an extremely hard nut that grows on the tagua tree. The lady in charge has a small lathe and can make them while you wait; her name is Maria, and I buy a very attractive necklace to take home. She is very happy to let me take a photograph of her and her young daughter.

The refreshment room is staffed by a lady called Martha, and as I drink my coffee she asks me about England: 'How far away is it? Is it very green? Is it expensive to live there?' I tell her that England is 7,000 miles away and that it took me many hours to get here.

She thinks that I must be very rich to be able to travel that far. I'm not sure, but at the end I think that she would rather stay in Alausi.

We have just left the station and on the outskirts of town we are having a run-by photograph over an impressive trestle bridge. The loco suddenly appears from between the houses and onto the bridge, and with a cloud of black smoke from its chimney it is an impressive sight. Because the train has started on a gradient there is a problem with the wheels not gripping, and I am treated to another sight that I would not see back home: one of the train crew is balanced on the front of the loco and is holding on with one hand while scooping sand from a box with the other and then putting it on the rails, all this while the train is in motion.

We have now been on the way for about an hour and have stopped to take on water and also have lunch; we are close to a very small mountain hamlet called Tixan. This is a very pleasant spot, with the mountains towering above us and alongside the railway a river tumbling over rocks on its way south. Stretched out on the grass under the warm sunshine I find very relaxing, and I idly watch the train crew taking the water pipe down to the river so that they can pump up water for the locomotive.

Miguel, the driver, is also looking very relaxed as he leans against the gently panting locomotive.

At the other side of the railway an Indian family have made their home. This is merely a lean-to under some trees. There is an area of cultivation and several animals including four donkeys, four cows, six dogs and some hens. I have shared my lunch with some of their children and this is both a rewarding and humbling experience. On this day sitting on the warm grass in this secluded valley and talking with them it seems an idyllic existence, but my snapshot view doesn't hide the fact that their existence in this lonely spot must be very hard at times.

We have now reached Tixan and there is a bit of a railway logjam. The gleaming railcar from Alausi has caught up with us and is anxious to get past; up ahead is our railcar, which is shadowing us for the entire journey. It's quite a procession.

Tixan is the point where the railway was more or less completely rebuilt following the extensive damage caused by El Nino in the early 1990s.

There is no such thing as signals or block working. It is all done by sight, hand and shouting, and we all move off until we reach a short rail spur some distance ahead. The railcar backs into this, and both our train and railcar reverse back so that he can proceed. The driver of the railcar does not look best pleased at being held up.

At Palmira summit, it is more that 10,000 feet above sea level and it is a bleak place. There is a small community built around the railway station and our train is soon surrounded by children.

Unlike many of the other places that we have stopped at, where the children and adults have been enthusiastic about our presence,

Palmira summit

here they merely display curiosity as they watch our arrival and departure.

From Palmira the track is both flat and straight for mile after mile as it follows the Andes plateau. The view is constant and is of black soil, tufts of brown grass, burnt tree stumps and the occasional conifer. In my notes I can see that I described this part of the journey as miles of nothingness.

It is a relief as we near Guamote and the countryside gradually changes from the black and lifeless-looking soil of the plateau to marsh land and then to green fields and rivers. There are now many areas of cultivation and the occasional Indian with the inevitable donkey.

We arrive in this traditional town about 4.30 p.m. and as the train comes to rest between shops and the station the whole scene looks as though it has not changed since the day that the railway first arrived here.

There is a woman cooking meat at a lineside stall over an extremely smoky fire, although the food does smell delicious. An old man is dozing under an awning outside a café, while a nearby Indian woman is wrapping her baby in the traditional way.

Lineside takeaway (Guamote)

She bends right over, lays the baby on her back and then wraps the shawl all around it so that it is totally covered; she then ties it around her neck and then straps it on with a white and purple strap. The bright green shawl goes right under the baby's bottom so that it is totally secure, and the finished product is a secure parcel with two little feet sticking out at the bottom.

A young man with what looks like an old-fashioned ice cream barrow is busily making drinks from various items and the contents of several bottles, although there are no customers that I can see.

After he has scraped the juice from a thick wide leaf and added all the other ingredients, he then pours the concoction from one jug to another and the finished product looks, to me, like thick brown slime.

The final product

I have written down the ingredients as he told me them:

Aloe
Una degato (cat's claw)
Chancapiedra (grass for kidneys)
Malt

Maca (protein source)
Natural honey
Fruit (*linaza* or linseed, and cinnamon)

When I ask him what the drink actually does, he says that it is a medication for all sorts of ills and ailments; I can't believe that I ask for a cupful of the mixture. It is very sweet and cloying but not unpleasant to drink, and I now look forward to a healthy completion of my journey through Ecuador.

There is a scene of some chaos in the station as two buses try to use the tracks to get in and out. There is a stationary railcar at the platform with a tanker on another line and our steam train on yet another track. To compound all this, a fault has developed with our locomotive and there is a freight train waiting to pass through the station. Everything works very well, even though it looks chaotic; there is no nonsense about signals or regulations or anything like that, and with a lot of arm-waving and horn-blaring from the locomotive the situation is rapidly sorted out.

From here we are going to Riobamba by coach, and the journey is through a wide open valley; this is the area where the Indians have been given all the land that used to belong to the rich landowners and they now work on it as a community. Some of the Indians have claimed the palatial haciendas of the former owners but they don't really live in them because they either don't know how, or they just don't like them; in consequence most of the buildings are falling into a serious state of disrepair.

On the way we make a brief stop in a small town called La Balbanera, the only point of interest here for us is the church which was built in 1534 and is the oldest in Ecuador; the Inca stones which form the base are very impressive as is the scroll work that still remains.

Tonight we are staying a few kilometres outside Riobamba in a sprawling hacienda where Simon Bolivar once stayed. Dominating this area is the mighty volcano of Chimborazo (6,310 metres) with

The oldest church in Ecuador

its permanent cap of snow, although it is wreathed in cloud at the moment. At one time explorers thought that Chimborazo was the highest mountain in the world, and although it has lost that honour, its summit is still the farthest point from the centre of the earth because of the earth's bulge at the equator. The bottom slopes of Chimborazo are very fertile and there are several tiny villages, where some of the farmers herd vicunas, deer-like animals much prized for their silky wool.

I have a very large room all to myself but I don't find it very welcoming.

There is very little lighting, and what bulbs there are appear to be very low wattage. The bed and furniture are big, heavy and of a dark wood and the overall effect is oppressive.

Needless to say I have a bad night, but whether this is psychological or for other reasons I don't know. The bonus for being up at dawn is a brilliant photograph of Chimborazo without a cloud and the snow glistening in the bright early morning sun.

*   *   *

Chimborazo

Guamote Station this morning is just as busy as yesterday and there are purveyors of all sorts of food and drink in and around the station.

At Guamote we are at just over 10,000 feet and for the first thirty kilometres between here and Cajabambawe the journey will be more or less level. This is demonstrated near the Colta Lagoon, where we make a stop in the middle of a very wide and flat green valley with a small stream meandering through it.

It's lunchtime! It can only be in South America where the train pulls up in the middle of nowhere and everybody then spends the next hour relaxing on the grass with sandwiches and drinks.

Colta Lagoon is a vast expanse of water that seems to go on and on. There are tall reed beds, and I can see a heron motionless at the water's edge; I can also see some white egrets. On the far side of the lagoon is the small town of Balbanera.

This part of the journey is very picturesque with the wide fertile green valley with Indians working and a small stream running

My lunchtime companion

through it. The surrounding hills are covered in eucalyptus trees and the sun is beating down.

The hustle and bustle of Riobamba is quite a contrast.

Few tourists reach this quintessentially Andean city with its population of about 140,000, and it is an easy city to find your way around. Following a devastating earthquake in 1797 the entire city was moved to its present site and the architecture is therefore neoclassical, except the cathedral, which was moved stone by stone and erected on its present site in the Parque Maldonado.

There are several places where you can get a view of the awe-inspiring Chimborazo volcano to the east, while to the south is Sangay volcano, which is one of the most active volcanoes in the world. The train journey between Riobamba and Quito runs through what is known as the 'Avenue of Volcanoes' with at least twelve volcanoes over 4,000 metres, including the famous Cotopaxi at 5,897 metres.

My stroll down 10 de Agosto takes me past another of Riobamba's several parks until I reach the market. This is an extremely colourful place with the Indian stallholders in their brightly-coloured clothes

It's been all go today

and their stalls piled high with vegetables, fruit and flowers. There is a vibrant atmosphere about the place, although not everybody is feeling it, as I can see two young Indian children fast asleep on the floor next to their mother.

I have a bit more time to visit the cathedral, which is a very impressive structure, all the more so when you consider how it got here.

Riobamba is a terminus station and there is a vast station yard with station buildings to match, and although the buildings are not in very good condition they are very obviously in the process of a significant refurbishment project.

There are only three lines in this huge yard, and they form into one at the entrance gate to the outside. The whole station area is fenced and gated from the roads and streets around it.

When you look at a map of the railway, Riobamba sits at the bottom of a V with the line to the left going to Alausi and the line to the right going to Quito. Trains for Quito have to reverse out of the station as far as the loco shed and workshops some distance away, they then take a separate line to Quito.

144

Leaving Riobamba

Today we are travelling the section from Riobamba to Urbina which, at 3,640 metres, lies close to the foot of Chimborazo.

The line from the station runs through a palm-fringed avenue with roads on each side and there are plenty of onlookers, some waving, some taking photographs (like me), and some just standing wondering what it is all about. There is a lot of black smoke and noise from the locomotive and everyone seems satisfied. All through the suburbs the route is lined with people waving, shouting and smiling. A pickup with several people in the back follows us for while, and although one woman stares steadfastly ahead, the rest are clearly having a wonderful time. It is very noticeable that although the houses on the edge of town are very poor-looking, being mostly unfinished brick and concrete, the people are, for the most part, very clean and smartly dressed, often with designer clothes.

We are now some way out of town and passing what resembles a prison. There is a high concrete wall with single-storey buildings all around the inside and an open concrete yard in the middle. On the outside of the wall in large red letters are the words

The Red Lantern

Bienvenidos Farol Rojo (Welcome to the Red Lantern). Although the pictures of nude women painted on the outside of the wall tend to give the game away, I still ask what this place is: 'a house of pleasure', I am told.

The line continues to climb, and we pass through green valleys and rolling hills where there is a lot of cultivation and neat and orderly villages. Further on near the summit it becomes much bleaker and colder and the cloud-shrouded mountains seem that much nearer. As we approach Urbina there is only poor-looking grass with a line of conifers and the solitary station building; but appearances are deceptive, for as we pull into the station a small crowd appears.

Urbina Station is a busier place than it first appears, for in addition to an occupied adjacent house, it also serves as a café and rest place for backpackers and walkers, and we have our lunch in a comfortable eating area inside. There are a group of llamas tethered on the other side of the line who are very suspicious of my intentions.

From Urbina, I track the train on its way back to Riobamba for a few miles by four-wheel drive and get a good opportunity

Urbina station

to photograph it crossing the old Pan-American Highway, with an Indian couple determined to beat the train across. No tarmac here; it is all linked grey stone sets, and the construction of this road must have taken years.

Racing the train

*   *   *

Another night at the hacienda, and we are now scheduled to make the complete run through to Quito from Riobamba, a distance of approximately 200 kilometres. Unfortunately, it turns out that we will only be able to travel about half the distance by rail because of problems with the track between Mocha and Latacunga, and the last piece between Tambillo and Quito is also closed due to road construction work that is affecting the railway. It means that there is a lot of railcar movement and travel by coach, and we are not able to enter Ambato or Latacunga by rail.

Ambato is a nice-looking but fairly modern town built on a series of hills with a lush green valley below and a brand new tarmac highway on the other side of the valley. It is about seventy-five miles from Quito, and like all the towns on this route, is surrounded by volcanoes, the nearest one being Tungu-rahua at 16,450 feet. The land in this area is very rich, and there is a centuries-old tradition of farming here. As in South American towns, a lot of the streets are named after famous people with names like Bolivar, Montalvo, Guayaquil, Benigno Vela and Maldonado.

Ambato's Fruits and Flowers Festival in February is one of the most popular carnivals in Ecuador.

Further on and some sixty miles from Quito is Latacunga, and just beyond is San Seren from where the railcar will take us on to Tambillo for the last rail leg of the G & Q, although there is a short trip from Ibarra still to come.

At Latacunga (9,000 feet) the railway is running alongside, and only yards from, the Pan-American Highway, and between that and the town is the Rio Cutuchi.

To the west of the railway station there are several small towns like Zumbahua, Chugchilan and Sigchosan with a patchwork of farms in between with fields of cacao and hay.

Latacunga lives under the shadow of Cotopaxi, the tallest active volcano in the world, and the town has been devastated on many occasions by its eruptions, although Cotopaxi has now been quiet for many years. All the eruptions of volcanic ash have meant that the soil is very rich with crops of sugar, coffee, fruit and cacao.

A national festival in Ecuador is Our Lady of Mercy Day on 24 September; this is especially celebrated in Latacunga, where there is a colourful parade presided over by Mama Negra, a mestizo dressed as a black woman, and followed by other characters such as the Angel of our Star, the King and the Flag Bearer.

Quito, and I have a day and a half to explore this very interesting city. My hotel is extremely nice, and at $80 (about £45) for bed and breakfast it is an absolute bargain, for that price I also get a suite!

There are two very attractive girls in reception, Anita and Yesenia, and they are both helpful, and keen to speak English.

Breakfast is quality with a wonderful selection of hot and cold food and a variety of fresh fruit and drinks. I have discovered something special for breakfast – a bowl of fresh pineapple chunks with walnuts and thick cream – and when I go for a second helping I tell myself that at least the fresh pineapple and nuts are good for me!

Quito is Ecuador's capital city and has a springtime climate throughout the year. It lies at 9,200 feet above sea level and is surrounded by towering green peaks that are usually shrouded in cloud. The city has a population of approximately 1.8 million and is divided into two parts, the New Town and the Old Town. The New Town is a thriving modern place with many high-rise buildings and is the social and commercial heart of Quito, while the Old Town has changed little since colonial days and is now the best preserved historic centre in Latin America. As such, UNESCO declared it a Cultural Heritage Site in 1978.

Life still revolves around the many plazas in the Old Town and there are a lot of splendid buildings. There are three large parks between the New Town (where I am staying) and the Old Town, and I decide to walk. On the way I meet a policeman called Alci, and it is an opportunity to practise my Spanish, as his English is not very good. He lives in Quito and is very proud of his city and its ancient buildings. He asks me if I am going to take (I didn't know the word, but we worked it out as chairlift) a trip to the top of Cruz Loma behind the Church of San Francisco. It is an enormously high mountain and I don't know whether I have the time, the bottle or the energy to do it. We'll see.

It is very pleasant walking through these parks but it is rather hot and I decide to take the trolleybus into the Old Town.

The trolleybus system in Quito is excellent. It runs from north to south the whole length of the city, and there are frequent bus stops where entry and exit is controlled. For 25c I can travel the entire length or just to the next stop. The buses are of the 'bendy' variety and they run on a dedicated route; it is an extremely cheap and efficient service.

There are many old and beautiful buildings and it is a pleasure to take photographs, especially with the many white buildings and the clear blue sky.

At the corner of Espejo and Avenue Guayaquil is the Bolivar Theatre. This was, at one time, an extremely grand theatre, but was ravaged by fire some years ago and there is currently restoration work going on. Even so, visitors are allowed into the foyer and the grand salon upstairs, but not into the auditorium. There are several photographs showing the extensive damage after the fire. There are magnificent columns which survive upstairs and the scrollwork is still ornate and magnificent, while downstairs the foyer with its marble floor is relatively untouched. It should be a wonderful sight when fully restored.

In the Plaza de la Independencia there is a very tall and ornate monument. It is a tribute to the heroes of 10 August 1809. The heroes were a group of natural and wealthy Ecuadorians who were planning a coup, but the Spanish found and a year later crushed the uprising and took them to the prisons under the building of the Jesuits, which is behind the cathedral, where they were later killed.

Plaza de la Independencia

All around the monument are the names of those captured and killed by the Spanish. That campaign is recognised as the first movement to independence by Ecuador, which actually followed twelve years later in 1822. The monument is very high, with a

The Monument

151

female figure on top symbolising independence and freedom. Near the base is a condor with outstretched wings and broken chains around its feet; this represents Ecuador and the gaining of its freedom, while at the base is a wounded lion, representing the Spanish who are defeated and going home.

In the same plaza is the cathedral, another beautiful old building with grey stone steps leading up to a vaulted entrance, behind which is the gleaming white bell tower. The cathedral was built in the sixteenth century and had a lot of changes and restoration following earthquakes of 1660 and 1797. Inside there is a small chapel that houses the remains of Mariscal Antonio José de Sucre, who commanded in the Battle of Pichincha and was a hero in the fight for Ecuadorian independence. The former currency of Ecuador was named after him.

Not far away is the Municipal Palace, I have wandered in here because it houses some pictures by one of Ecuador's most famous modern artists. His name was Endara Crow and he was a surrealist painter who liked to depict the old town and also butterflies and hummingbirds. I am looking at a very large painting that he

Endara Crow's picture

completed in 1986. It depicts the old town with the largest church and the presidential palace against a backdrop of the Andes and Cotopaxi volcano.

Across a deep blue sky he has depicted a train with first-class coaches and a flat wagon on which people are sitting. There is a stream of fiery smoke coming from the chimney of the locomotive and I have learned that he always included a train in his paintings.

All the plazas and important buildings in the old town are immaculate, and buildings like the cathedral, the Presidential Palace and San Francisco convent with their gleaming white facades, look an absolute picture against the bright blue sky.

Behind the statue of independence is the Presidential Palace, a long building taking up a whole side of the Plaza Grande. Above the main square and for the full length of the building is a covered walkway with plain grey stone pillars.

The presidential guard are on duty and there is one on each side of the entrance. With their black jackboots, white trousers, red and blue jackets with matching helmets and gold braids they are an impressive sight; each of them is holding a twelve-foot-long spear.

At plaza level on the wall there is a plaque to indicate that this was the spot where Dr Gabriel Garcia Moreno was assassinated on 6 August 1875 by a man wielding a machete. Dr Moreno was President of Ecuador and also founder of the Ecuadorian rail system.

During my wanderings, I had seen a statue on top of a hill high above the Old Town. I have now decided to investigate and am being driven up a long, winding and tortuous road.

The journey is worth it, for high above Quito is El Panecillo, known as Yavirac before the arrival of the Spanish. This was a ritual area for sun worship, and legend has it that before the arrival of the Spanish, the Inca priests used the area at the top as a place to pay homage to the sun at the Sun Festival (*Intyi Raymi*) on 24 June.

At the top there is an aluminium statue one hundred feet high that is a reproduction of Legarda's 'Virgin' in San Francisco church. There is also a permanent market where you can buy all manner of handicrafts, and I haggle for a delightful blue poncho as a present to take home. The girl that sells it to me is called Luce Maria and she is delighted to model it for me.

The view from up here is amazing, with all of Quito spread out at your feet.

Legarda's Virgin

It has been a hot and tiring day and I have decided to return to the hotel for a quiet drink and something to eat before an early night, as tomorrow there is another two days' travelling to visit Peguche, Otavalo and Ibarra, before I return to Quito for a further two days.

Wanting something quick and easy, I opt for a fast-food place just around the corner from the hotel, and although the decor is a bit basic it is clean enough and will do me for tonight.

From the set menu, I order half a chicken and chips with rice and bean sauce for $2.50. Before it arrives I am a bit surprised to be served with a bowl of chicken and vegetable soup, and a drink of lemonade; it turns out that this comes free with the particular meal that I have ordered.

The soup, although a bit thin, is quite tasty and there is a lot of it, and plenty of vegetables as well. I enjoy the first few spoonfuls and then see what appears to be a piece of chicken lurking at the bottom … but when I lift it with my spoon, it turns out to be the complete claw of a chicken! It has that white wrinkled look of a body that has been in the water for a long time.

Perhaps it is the spirit of South America, but I don't view this culinary novelty with the disgust and horror that I might have done at home and merely put the bowl on one side and wait for my main order. My only disappointment was not having my digital camera with me to record what was certainly a unique gastronomic experience for me.

Today there is a long drive to Ibarra; this is because the section of line from Quito to Ibarra is not operational, owing to landslips. From Ibarra the line used to continue to the coast but this section is also broken, and from Ibarra we will only be able to travel towards the coast for approximately forty kilometres towards Primer Paso, and this only by rail car.

At the end of this account of my journey I have listed details of the sections of the entire Guayaquil-Quito-Ibarra-San Lorenzo line that are still open, and although the route is very fragmented it is still worth the trip; but for how much longer it will be possible is anybody's guess.

On the journey there are several typical South American towns that sprawl on each side of the road, and as we pass through one of them I notice a restaurant on the outskirts where the advertising is aggressive, if not enticing. Not for them a billboard but a wooden structure not unlike a gallows. Hanging from the crossbar is a full-size and very lifelike plaster pig. It is suspended by its neck with its stomach slit open and the contents showing red. It is now two months later, and I still cannot bring myself to eat pork!

We are now running down a large and very green valley and in the distance I can see Ibarra, from here the buildings look very white.

The train journey from Ibarra is tomorrow and tonight we stay in the Hosteria Chorlavi, five kilometres from Ibarra.

Although it is now nearly dark, there is enough light to see that the Hosteria Chorlavi is an attractive place, and was once a hacienda of some consequence. The approach is down a long mimosa-lined drive which opens out onto a large forecourt, with the Hosteria nestling under large palm trees. The long, low veranda in front, on which there are some very attractive and probably antique chairs, looks very inviting.

I am sure that dinner was very nice but it passes me by a bit and I am glad to turn in for an early night. The bedroom is all big heavy furniture in a small room. There is no hot water, but who cares – it's got a bed.

There is only time for breakfast in the morning before we are on our way, so I am up at 6 a.m. to have a look round. My room looks out on the back and outside my window there is a deep ravine with a stream at the bottom and a lot of lush greenery; a picturesque little bridge takes you over to a large lawn with two enormous palm trees from which are strung two hammocks.

It is a beautiful warm morning and I am lying, gently swaying, in one of the hammocks watching birds. There's a beautiful all black bird with a red chest, a very small bird about the size of a robin, which is brilliant red all over, and a hummingbird feeding from a group of pink flowers.

Breakfast calls and it is nearly time to go. What a pity…

Ibarra at 9.30 a.m. on a beautiful sunny day with a cloudless

Ferrocarril Quito San Lorenzo

blue sky. First stop is the workshop and rail yard. The workshop is a long white building with nine sets of tracks running into it. On the front of the building in shiny blue letters is the legend, Ferrocarril Quito San Lorenzo.

The incredible thing about this place is that it employs sixty people and they don't have anything to do!

There are two big modern diesels, several old diesels, some railcars and a steam loco, together with a very modern and well-equipped workshop and loco shed ... and no use for the locos except for the occasional charter trip with a railcar.

There is much talk about the opening of the full length of the line to San Lorenzo on the coast 200 kilometres away, but at the moment it is only open as far as El Paso, about forty kilometres away. We were scheduled to do the first five kilometres behind a steam loco but now the whole trip will be by railcar; a bit of a let-down, really.

To alleviate our disappointment, it has been arranged that the steam loco (Baldwin, No. 14, 2–6–0) will take us through town to the station and back before our trip to El Paso. No carriages

Ibarra station and extra passengers!

for this short journey, it is either sit on a flatbed truck or ride on the roof; nothing wrong with either option, really. It seems as though the whole town has turned out for this event. Traffic has stopped and the streets are lined with onlookers.

There is a woman sitting in a chair doing her knitting and smiling and nodding at us as we pass. She could almost be counting heads next to the guillotine!

As we slowly trundle through the town I find it very refreshing to see that it is not cluttered up with fences stopping you walking on the road or crossing here, or not crossing there, and all sorts of other restrictions about this that and the other. People here make their own choices about how they go about their day-to-day life in the town without having to be regimented by signs and warnings.

We are suddenly halted in the middle of a road crossing and the whole train is immediately surrounded with traffic and pedestrians. It is like a signal, and suddenly the whole train is covered in people. There is not an inch of space on the flatbed trucks, and the boxcar roofs are also covered in people, with some hanging on to the edge, with their feet dangling towards the track. I can see at least ten people sitting on the engine tender as well, and as we move off towards the station it is a remarkable sight with the train like a moving island of people inching its way through a positive sea of humanity.

The sign in Ibarra Station says that it is 2,210 metres (7,250

The day that the train came to Ibarra

feet) above sea level and 173 kilometres to Quito and 200 kilometres to San Lorenzo.

Despite all the hustle and bustle, there is timelessness about Ibarra. A great mountain looms just beyond the town with snowy white clouds drifting across its peak; the mountain has an almost protective air towards the little town and its people that nestle at its foot in this remote corner of Ecuador, not far from the Colombian border.

It is 11 a.m. and we are now just running out of Ibarra with the mountains very clear and sharp around us. The sky is a bright blue and although there is now quite a bit of cloud it is very hot.

We are now clear of the town and it is very green and attractive with bright red hibiscus bushes and pink oleanders. There are also rows and rows of yucca trees with their brilliant white flowers, interspersed with cactus bushes with bright red pompom flowers on the top, and nearby there is a little community with some cattle lazily grazing.

We are passing through a very fertile area and there is a lot of cultivation here, with crops of cabbages, broccoli, beans, lettuce and onions. I have to be very careful about leaning out of the window at this point as there are huge cactuses alongside the railway, and their razor sharp stems could inflict a very serious wound. There are some beautiful butterflies and their yellow, brown and gold colouring sparkles in the sunlight as they flit from flower

159

to flower. They are about twice the size of any butterfly that you would see in the UK. A big black bird flaps lazily overhead; it looks like a crow but it is much larger.

We have moved on a few kilometres and the surrounding scenery is now much more rugged, although close to the railway it is still very green. This is because there is a small stream alongside the railway and not only is the track covered in grass in many places, it is also underwater in others!

It is fascinating to see bromeliads growing seemingly everywhere; they are fastened onto trees and also onto telegraph wires.

The railway is now very much part of the mountains and the track clings to the edge in many places. We are just going to cross a bridge and will do a run-by photo session here and I can't resist quoting exactly from my taped notes at this point, although the written word doesn't convey the feeling that was in my voice at the time: 'We are just going to cross a bridge – a run-by, I bet. My God, it's bloody high as well!'

There is a river far below and on the other side of the bridge the track disappears into a tunnel.

The Bridge

On the other side of the gorge that we are passing through there have been huge landslips and I can see where two great swathes of the mountain have just dropped down into the river.

The line is continuing to cling to the cliff edge, and far below us in the valley I can see signs of cultivation and more crops.

We have now been running in a deep cutting for some time and there is a small stream again running alongside us. As we come out of the cutting the line is again perched on a ledge above a deep gorge with matching mountains on the other side.

Far below, I can see channelled water with a pumping station and a small settlement. It is very high at this point. A little further on and we are now passing through a series of tunnels; there is only a short distance between them and I wonder about the head clearance for the two people travelling on the roof.

Suddenly we pass an abandoned station; it is quite a sight, high up in this desolate and lonely place without a single house or a person for miles, although far below us there is a dirt track road, also winding its way through tunnels.

From the mountain on the other side of the gorge I can see a waterfall falling hundreds of feet to the valley below.

It is a very desolate place here with dead-looking trees and even dead-looking cactuses. Then without warning the line is suddenly running away from the cliff edge and there are acres and acres of sugar cane between the railway and the cliff edge. It is an almost brutal contrast. A short while ago we were clinging to the side of a cliff and now there is a wide open valley with fertile fields and trees. There is also more sugar cane. On the far side of the valley there are fires burning on the mountain where the Indians are burning off the scrub so that they can plant their crops.

On a bend in the middle of nowhere we have a derailment. It is very hot. This situation is obviously old hat for the train crew, as

General views from Ibarra to El Paso

after fifteen minutes with a car jack and a couple of pieces of wood we are on our way.

It is now some four hours since we left Ibarra and the line is again perched on the side of a cliff. The contrast between running through fertile green valleys and clinging to unstable rock faces is quite startling.

We have only gone a couple of kilometres and I can hear small stones falling on the roof from the cliff above; on the other side I can see small stones and dirt being dislodged by the movement of our passing and falling into the valley far below.

This part of the journey makes the rest of the Ecuadorian rail system seem quite tame. It was an incredible feat of engineering to drive this line through these enormous mountains. I am looking back at them now, and when you see them it seems incredible that anybody even thought about building this line, let alone doing it.

There is another halt, this time for a rock fall across the line, and we all muck in to clear the track. It is a bit disconcerting that scree continues to fall on the line as we work.

It's a hell of a long walk if we get stuck here, but my pessimism is not rewarded.

The line is now again perched high on the side of the mountain and as we pass I can see dirt falling from the 'pebbly'-looking mountain side as a result of the vibration of our passing. Looking

162

Volunteers needed

to the other side of the gorge I can see several areas where great chunks of hillside have come down, and when you see them you think that it can only be a matter of time before this and other sections of the Ecuador rail system are swept away for ever by the forces of nature. This is surely the price of deforestation.

Clouds are now coming in and covering the tops of the mountains.

There is another short stop to pick stones off the line, and minutes later I can hear dust and stones falling on the roof of the railcar. We are passing through more tunnels that have been hewn out of the mountain, I have lost count, but there must have been at least twenty since we left Ibarra.

The view looking back is incredible. We have been following this towering mountain range by means of an unbelievably narrow ledge interspersed with tunnels and it is an incredible engineering feat. There are very few straight pieces of track and the wheel flanges are continually squealing against the rails as we twist and turn with the contours of the mountain.

We have now dropped down drastically in height and have suddenly crossed the road that had been following us along the

The last bridge

bottom of the valley hundreds of feet below. The road is obviously a main route and is extremely good quality, with smooth tarmac and white lines. It forms a harsh contrast with the state of the railway track and is, I am sure, another omen about the future of this railway.

We are nearly at the point where the line has been washed away, and as we cross the road the surroundings are just cactuses, dead trees, dust and grey and brown mountains.

We have just emerged from yet another tunnel only this one leads straight onto a bright yellow girder bridge, over a river that is rushing on its way over smooth polished grey stones.

The end of the line, at approximately forty-four kilometres from Ibarra, is just a few yards away.

Time for lunch and photos.

On either side the mountains tower above us, and although the sound of rushing water from the river close by is very pleasant, it is extremely hot and even the shade of a dead and withered tree is welcome. There are some abandoned houses and one that it still inhabited. A dog eyes me suspiciously and chickens forage in

The end of the line, literally

the dust. A little further on is the actual end of the line; one of the many ravines that split the mountains leads straight down to the line and a flood has brought down a wall of earth, stones and rubble and buried the rails. Although the rails are not buried very deep, the surrounding ground has been undermined and made unstable.

It is time to go and there is a dust-covered turntable that is just big enough for the railcar, but it is hot work pushing it round by hand!

We are now on the way back, and after crossing the tarmac road have climbed about another 300 feet when there is suddenly a grinding noise and the railcar rocks and tilts over slightly. We have derailed again and have been very lucky not to overturn.

Two feet from the railcar is a 300-foot drop and we have been fortunate indeed not to go over the edge. This time the derailment is a bad one and the crew will have to send to Ibarra for assistance. It is arranged for the coach that has been shadowing us to pick us up at the road crossing, and it is a hot and dusty hike back down the track.

A near thing

We are now back in Ibarra for the final bit of rail travel, which is a short trip through town to the rail depot. It is very much a photo shoot, and again there are hundreds of people joining in the fun and the flatbed wagons are full to overflowing. A plastic chair has appeared from somewhere and there is an elderly gentleman sitting in it smoking a pipe and looking for all the world like a statesman awaiting the introduction of guests.

People are taking all sorts of chances to get onto the wagons while they are moving, and one young woman throws her small daughter to me to catch while she scrambles on. She slips, and I end up grabbing one leg and one arm and hauling her aboard. Her name is Sereta and she is twenty-five years old. Her children are Priscilla and Camilla and she has brought them today because they have not seen anything like this before.

After a group photo in the rail yard, it is time to head back to the Hosteria Chorlavi to write up my notes, have dinner and an early night before tomorrow, which is scheduled to be a long coach trip back to Quito, calling at Otavalo, Peguche and Cotacachi on the way.

It is another fine day and the forecourt of the Hosteria is a blaze of colour. There is a large sprawling pink and orange plant called lantana, a pale blue creeper, bright red hibiscus trees, bright yellow potentilla-type bushes and pale pink oleanders. In some places they have all grown so thickly that they have been cut into a hedge.

The soft seat in the coach is quite a change from the seating in the railcar, and while relaxing to enjoy the view I can see a huge covered area where flowers are grown for export. This is a major trade for Ecuador.

We have passed through a few small towns; they are all much the same in Ecuador in that they sprawl along each side of the road that runs through them, when suddenly at the roadside there is what seems to be a thriving business selling figures for your garden. The difference here is that, although you can buy Greek statues, Roman soldiers, elephants, cows, men with tridents, and even reproductions of famous Ecuadorian people, they are all life-size!

We are nearing Otavalo and have just turned off the main road, and the coach is now threading its way up a steep rough road to the town of Peguche, noted for its weaving.

We are now in the main plaza of Peguche; it is a very neat and tidy sprawling grey town with houses and shops around the plaza. It's very quiet; perhaps the heat is keeping people indoors.

First stop is to see inside a typical family home where people share their accommodation with their animals. The floor is of packed earth and there are guinea pigs running around everywhere.

It is also a working home, and a man and a woman are producing scarves, pullovers, mats and other fabric items on very primitive-looking equipment, there is however nothing primitive about the prices that they are asking for their wares!

There is a little time to explore and I am now outside a large house called Parada (built in 1613). This was an area of slavery and Parada House is now a kindergarten taking care of children. It is the Foundation for Lost Indigenous Children.

We are heading for the Bosque Protector Cascada de Peguche (Protected Forest and Waterfall of Peguche), and along the way I have stopped to photograph an Inca calendar made up of stones set in the ground.

We have entered the woodland area where there are a lot of beautiful flowers and shrubs, together with eucalyptus and indigenous trees that tower their way to the sky in a dead straight line.

It is neither hot nor cold walking through this woodland, and then suddenly you see the waterfall emerging from the misty air.

Peguche Waterfall

It is a spectacular sight, and from the clear pool at its base a man-made trough takes the water on a journey, presumably for irrigation.

We have taken the short drive to Cotacachi, stopping on the way for a coconut ice cream (delicious).

168

Cotacachi is famous for its leather, and is indeed the leather-work capital of Ecuador. Here you can buy almost anything in leather and the prices are very reasonable.

The road into town is a rough and narrow street with some very poor-looking houses and there are a lot of school children about. Here, as everywhere in Ecuador, they are extremely smartly dressed.

The change in the middle of the town is quite dramatic, with paved and spotlessly clean streets, very smart shops and an impressive cathedral with an imposing sweep of steps to its entrance.

The happy man of Cotacachi who gave my shoes a shine

The main plaza and its town nestle under Mount Cotacachi (4,939 metres) which today has thick white clouds rolling over its peak, although the town is bathed in lovely hot sunshine.

The plaza is made up of triangles of garden with palm trees and shrubs and is a very enticing place to sit and people-watch. Although there are very few of them about, it is a very relaxing here and I find it difficult to motivate myself for the next part of the journey to Otavalo.

Cotacachi

As we leave town we pass another plaza, and in a small piece of fenced garden there are three statues of more than life-size. One man is working leather on a bench, and the others are a pan pipes player and a violinist: music while you work.

Otavalo (2,566 metres) is an interesting mixture. It is a prosperous and respected indigenous community where the people speak Quechua on the street, wear traditional dress and produce beautiful weaving and music that is recognised worldwide.

On the other hand, Otavalo has also widened its talent, and many of the population are also professionals such as lawyers, doctors and politicians. The town has accepted some Western values and technology but remains firmly traditional.

The famous market is much more than a tourist stop. It is an experience, with its bewildering array of goods for sale including carvings, tapestries, paintings, leatherwork, jewellery and handmade pipes. Traditional dress is worn everywhere and the colour and spectacle of the scene is exciting.

The town is embraced to the north and south by the Pan-American Highway, and from the Poncho Plaza, where the main part of the market is, it is not more than 200 or 300 yards in any direction to explore the town centre. It is very little different from other small towns that I have seen so far, but it undoubtedly bursts out and expresses itself in its market.

Down one of the side streets I am tempted by the smell of roast pork, and after a cultural exchange with the vendor, I continue my

170

ramble with a small bag of hot pork pieces. A sign outside a café is advertising a drink called Guayusu. It looks interesting, and when I found out later that it was very potent drink made from fermented sugar cane and lemon, I felt a twinge of regret for not trying it.

I am now thinking of presents for home and here I find one that I have been looking for – a bronze statue of Atahualpa.

A present for another son is an Ecuadorian National Team football shirt, about eighty per cent cheaper than in the UK!

It is time to leave this interesting little town and head for Quito and my last full day in Ecuador.

I am staying in the same luxurious hotel and having already spent a day and a half in Quito, today is going to be a day of mainly relaxation before the long trip home.

I have planned to visit La Mitad del Mundo this morning, and this afternoon will be mainly spent people-watching from one of the street cafés along Avenue Amazonas.

I have been told that the journey to Mitad del Mundo takes about forty minutes on the bus, so I intend to take a taxi there and return on the bus. I have negotiated a fare of $10, which I am later told was very reasonable.

The taxi driver asks me if I mind if we stop for petrol, and as he fills up, I idly watch two men joining up a long hose, with clips and tape, to the nozzle of a petrol pump. It appears that they are transferring petrol from an underground tank to the pump, but the smell of gasoline on the forecourt is overpowering and I am sure that one spark would blow us all away.

The journey takes forty-five minutes so the time I was given for the bus was certainly a bit optimistic.

Mitad del Mundo is on the outskirts of San Antonio de Pichincha and is where, in 1736, a French scientist called Charles Marie de La Condamine (1701–1774) determined the exact location of the equatorial line that divides the planet into north and south. The monument is made of grey stone blocks and is about one

171

hundred feet high, with a large and well-detailed world globe on the top.

It is set in the middle of a very attractive park and the long paved pathway from the entrance is lined with the busts of famous men from France, Spain and Ecuador who explored the equator from 1736 to 1744.

There is a charge of $1.50 to the site, but it is money well spent as there is a lot to see and it is easy to spend a couple of hours here with shops, museums, restaurants, cafés and other displays, including a miniature model of Old Quito, Cuenca and Guayaquil. The whole park is spotlessly clean.

Mitad del Mundo

This seems to be a wonderful place to buy my granddaughter's birthday present, and from a little shop I buy a charming little green poncho decorated with llamas, cactuses and the sun. These are sold to me by Christiana Rosa, who is shy and friendly in equal measure, and during our conversation she tells me that she makes these little ponchos herself.

From the monument an orange line, denoting the equator, runs through the whole complex, even down the middle of the aisle of a newly-built church.

The little green poncho

It is two hours later and I am on a bus back to town. It is an interesting journey as I am the only European on the bus, and although I am quite clearly of no interest to many of the passengers, some of them stare at me continually, including two little boys of about five and a girl of about eight who are sitting next to me. It is as though they cannot believe the sight of a gringo on this bus full of indigenous people!

The passengers are a wonderful mixture with Indians, children in track suits, unkempt men in unkempt suits and a few smartly dressed people with briefcases.

A sign says 'Capacity 40 seated and 10 standing' but there are at least twenty-five people standing, and although it is stiflingly hot in here, nobody seems to want a window open. To add to the atmosphere, there is music roaring out over speakers.

Just as I am beginning to feel a little light-headed, the bus comes to a stop and everybody gets off. I have no idea why, but when I ask I am told that this is the terminus for the outlying buses and we are now transferring to the trolleybus system for the rest of the journey into the city. It has been a most entertaining ride so far.

The ticket that I bought at Mitad del Mundo for 40c includes both bus rides, and I can see from my notes that the return journey took just over an hour: what a bargain!

The rest of the ride on this trolleybus is exhilarating. These bendy buses have a seating capacity of forty-eight and a standing capacity of eighty, and my bus is full to that limit. The driver also seems to want to go as fast as possible on his dedicated route between the lines of other traffic.

I manage to get a seat next to him and he is very friendly and happy to talk about his beloved city, and he is delighted about someone from England wanting to visit his country.

Although the journey seems more hair-raising from up front, we are soon in the city and he drops me off at the Parque de El Ejido (the 'park of common land').

This is a beautiful and spacious park with large areas of grass, trees and shrubs. It is very hot, but nice and cool under the shade of the trees. Young couples on the grass lie in each other's arms, oblivious of everything. A large group of people are watching a man do magic tricks. A man with a briefcase stands scratching his head and looking about him. A group of young girls are sitting in a circle talking quietly, and every so often one of them gives a shriek of laughter. Three police horses are gently cropping the grass under some large trees; there is no sign of the policemen. An old man in a faded suit and waistcoat sits on a bench, basking in the warmth of the sun; he nods and smiles at all the passers-by.

Parque de El Ejido

All the travelling of the last three weeks has brought me to this – an oasis of pleasure, enjoyment and relaxation in the middle of this busy and beautiful city.

Here, time seems of no importance and I feel as though I could sit on this bench for ever, watching the ebb and flow of life around me.

It is now late afternoon and I am sitting at a street café on Avenue Amazonas drinking coffee and watching life go by.

A young boy hovers nearby and whenever the waiter is not looking he darts in to one of the tables and offers a shoeshine to the customer. Sometimes his timing is bad and the waiter chases him off, but he continues to hover on the pavement.

Amazonas is the main shopping street for tourists in Quito, and you can buy virtually anything Ecuadorian there, at a price. Ecuador is also where Panama hats are made, not Panama.

It seems that other things are available as well, as I am currently the object of attention of a tall, dark-skinned young woman, who walks past my table, smiles and disappears down the street. A few moments later the shoeshine boy sidles up and gives me a tiny scrap of paper with the name Dianita and a telephone number on it.

The atmosphere in the street is changing, and there are now street sellers everywhere. They are all selling the same things: flags, scarves, horns and banners. Tomorrow, at the Atahualpa Stadium in Quito, Ecuador are playing Uruguay in a match that will decide which of them will be going to the 2006 World Cup matches in Germany, and the city is suddenly electric with excitement. I have seen some of the passion of South American football but only on television, and to be part of that passion is quite an experience. Televisions in shops and takeaways are showing nothing else except opinions and predictions for the game tomorrow. A man staggers past, completely engulfed in flags and banners, while another is pushing a bicycle on which there are strings of horns, rather like strings of onions. It is very difficult to be neutral here tonight.

Lying in bed later before my long flight home in the morning, I can't help feeling that today has neatly summed up Ecuador for me. It has, in turn, been beautiful, exciting, breathtaking, passionate, peaceful, vibrant and above all else, welcoming.

Appendix I

Operational information about the Ecuadorian Railway System, as at October 2005

- Duran Station closed; trains now leave from Duran loco shed.
- Duran to Yaguachi: still operating, steam and railcar.
- Yaguachi to Bucay closed. No rails at Milagro.
- Bucay to Huigra, still operating but only with a railcar.
- Huigra to Sibambe closed. Landslip.
- Sibambe to Alausi, still operating, steam and railcar.
- Alausi to Mocha, still operating.
- Mocha to San Seren (Latacunga) closed. Landslip.
- Latacunga to Tambillo, still operating, but only with a railcar.
- Tambillo to Quito closed. Road works but scheduled to reopen.
- Quito to Ibarra section closed.

Operational information about the Ibarra to San Lorenzo Railway, as at October 2005

- Ibarra westward open, but only for approximately forty-four kilometres. Railcar only.
- San Lorenzo eastward open, but only for approximately eighty kilometres. Railcar only.

Appendix II

Details of the busts at La Mitad del Mundo

- Antonio de Ulloa 1716–1795
- Gorge Juan Santacilia 1713–1773
- Gublet 1686–1737
- Godin des Odonnais 1712–1780
- Morainville 1706–1774
- Hogot 1694–1743
- Joseph de Jussieu 1704–1779
- Seniergue 1684–1739
- Vergiuin 1704–1770
- Pierre Borguier 1693–1758
- Louis Godin 1704–1774
- Charles Marie de la Condamine 1701–1774